With A Little Faith

With A Little Faith

2nd Edition

Jude Stringfellow

"Now faith is the substance of things hoped for, the evidence of things unseen."

Hebrews 11:1

To order additional copies of this book, contact:
Xlibris Corporation
1-888-795-4274
www.Xlibris.com
Orders@Xlibris.com
34958

Contents

Dedicated to Mom and Dad. They've been kissing each other for more than 50 years.

DISCLAIMER

At times, I felt it necessary to change the names of not only the guilty, but the innocent as well. At times, my friends asked me to change their names and this begs the question: Are they innocent or guilty? You decide. My brother has asked me if I have told the entire truth while writing the book, and I must say, that after reading it I can find two tales which are not all together truthful, but I'm not telling you which ones they are, thus giving me an out should I need one. Happy reading.

Thank You Page

I greatly thank anyone and everyone who helped me to get this book published by sending me donations from your heart. There are a few who need to be mentioned by name and they are: Ginger and Dennis Handy of Tennessee, who first read my inquest and responded immediately. Secondly, I wish to thank Ericka from Seattle, Washington, who not only showed tremendous faith by sending me a donation, she's a student who works part time at a hospital just to make ends meet. Thank you BIG TIME to Debbie Minshall, her husband and her two sons Matt and Evan. I met Debbie and the boys at the Harry Potter 6 party at Borders of Oklahoma City on July 15, 2005. Debbie and I talked briefly about the book, and she was so inspired about the idea, she literally paid every penny I had left to pay on the publishing costs. You can say what you want to say, but people are out there who want to make a difference. Thank you guys so much for your help.

Prologue

I was sitting there reading the latest cartoon captions of *Todd the Dinosaur*, minding my own business, because that is what I always do, and my son came into the house with that "look" on his face. He was smiling. He wasn't going to tell me why, but I knew that in the 17 years I had known him that there were very few reasons for this particular smile. Funny isn't it? I can tell which of my children has let gas in the closed car by the smell, it doesn't matter how well you've trained them, they all do it, and I find it a little disturbing that I can detect with just my nostrils which of my kids to blame. I'm never wrong . . . this smile, this barely showing the teeth, but all the dimples being exposed for optimal cuteness. What was he about to do? What was I about to get myself into? It was always unexpected and it was always unavoidable. In a flash my life would be changed. "It was true Mom", he began without missing an opportunity to look me square in the eyes, "Princess had a bunch of puppies and she had some of them without legs and one died because it couldn't fight off the others. Another one died when it walked into the snow I guess, and she didn't go out and get it. I found it, I buried it." A tragic story yes, but he hadn't stopped the excessive smiling. That's when it hit me. No! He didn't! He knows we can't have another dog in this house! We already broke the rules with Matrix, a beagle-dachshund mix that we had re-rescued from the shelter just a month before. Our landlord Frank would have my head if he thought we went out and got another dog.

It wasn't the first time, Reuben had already stepped over the line (again) when he had to have a cat, and when one cat comes another one finds its way into my house. I was already being asked to pay more each month to cover the deposit on the animals that Frank had been so adamant about—adamant in that we couldn't have any. We had Matrix, but for some reason Frank believed me when I told him he would be staying down the street with friends. "You didn't bring home one of those dogs Reuben!" I protested. I stomped my right foot, slammed down the dish towel in my hands, which I had been using to dry dishes before picking up Patrick Roberts' *Todd* cartoon. Reu was suppose to have washed hours ago. "You did not bring home a puppy just because she had too many. Oh my gosh Reuben, it was only two weeks ago! You can't bring a two-week old puppy here and expect it to live, its mother has to feed it, it doesn't even have its eyes open I'm sure." I continued protesting. I know I did, and there he was, smiling. While he wouldn't stop showing off those dimples, he reached into the folds of his football jersey, pulling out the fuzziest, yellowest, cutest little pointed-earred puppy I had ever seen . . . . without front legs. This was going to take a little faith!

PART ONE

Family

Chapter One

It wasn't as if I woke up one sunny day and decided to divorce my husband, go back to school, lose my job, and raise a two-legged dog. I'm quite aware of how it may seem to some as they read this book that this is what must have happened; however, I assure you I was one of those people who believed in staying married even if the guy I was married to wound up being the biggest jerk on the face of the planet. I had actually divorced him twice because my morality was such that I felt that I simply had to give him every chance possible. OK . . . having done that, and having been paid back in ways that will not only confuse and dumbfound you, the reader, I begin this story by backing up from the main topic of the book long enough to establish what it is that our family went through, and why the dog we call "Faith" is so endearing to us. It isn't simply because she is perhaps the most unique and unusual animal I have ever met, it is also because our family had been through so much before she came along; her coming to us at the moment in our lives when we most needed her was nothing short of a miracle.

I love my kids. I really love my kids. If I had to do the kid thing all over again, I would no doubt let my friend Denzel raise them. They would have turned out so very differently, and probably for the better. Denzel has a kinder, more intellectual view of the world. He would know just exactly where to place my children in his garden of life. I call my son Reuben the joy of my heart because he never ceases to surprise me. At every turn in my life he finds a way to jump start me into sheer terror, enthusiasm, surrealism, or some other emotion which causes my face to stretch into endless facial contractions; he can be such a loving and giving child, while at the very same time, he can be so brutally honest it leaves me dropping my jaw in embarrassment as he makes an announcement to the world which could very well have been kept private. At the age of two he bent himself over, pulled down his pants exposing his bum, only to tell the crowded auditorium at the Governor's Christmas party that he had wiped himself by himself . . . so proud! At ten he hit a baseball so hard it slammed into the chest of the pitcher on the other team, knocking the boy to the ground immediately. Because Reuben is so "Reuben", he never ran to first base; instead he ran directly to the kid laying on the mound, lifted him up into his arms, rocking him and trying to bring him back to consciousness. Naturally, he was thrown out at first base. I couldn't have been more impressed with my son than I was at that moment. It was Reuben who actually held me in his arms at the age of fifteen when the District Court Judge made a monumental error during a custody battle revoking my rights as the custodial parent. The error was obvious to anyone who had actually taken the time to read the case file; yet the judge refused to be corrected publicly. I fell hard to the ground in what must have been one of my few completely uncontrolled moments. I can never forget the day, or the moment when my future and the future of my two daughters was suspended without reason. I had gone to court with evidence which would show not only a preponderance of guilt on the part of my former spouse, but physical evidence that his wife had physically hurt my daughter Laura. I had left medical and taped evidence with my attorney, what could have gone wrong?

Once the hearing began I wasn't allowed to speak. My attorney had not surrendered the evidence on time, my own counsel had not taken the time to do his job, which in turn gave the Judge the impression that I was negligent in fulfilling my obligations as a parent. What was worse, if I'm not mistaken, was that the Judge had believed that it was I who had left bruises and contusions on my daughter's arm. She believed it was me who had held my daughter to the ground and spat on her. No, it wasn't me. I couldn't comprehend what was going on right in front of me. My voice was silenced, my evidence unannounced. In a moment I was hearing the Judge's announcement that I was being banished from my daughters and that I would have my visitation rights suspended unless they were supervised. This wasn't suppose to happen. I was the one saving them from the monsters they were being hurt by. Nothing made sense, and my county paid counsel wasn't making it make any sense to the Judge. I later found out that he had not even brought the correct file to court. This was not the first time an attorney had misplaced my file and I was the one punished for their mistake. For over three years this battle of sole custody had raged and my former spouse, their father, had managed to evade the court's true and correct ruling. Whatever trick he had played, whatever false document he had managed to file or have his attorney file, it was working.

Everything went blank, the room felt black, swirling with confusion and upheaval as my attorney tried to reckon with the Judge over his mistake. He wasn't willing to take the blame for not being prepared, but he did at least state that the evidence he would have brought would have proved our point. I heard the words and I realized that my girls were forever banned from me. I hit the ground, I hit the ground hard. The next thing I remember as I lay feeling nothing at all, seeing dust under the benches in the crowded court room was my son Reuben as he carefully reached down literally picking me up, rocking me in his arms. He held me so tightly, and he sweetly told me "It's going to be OK, Mom, it's going to be OK." This is my son; he is the joy of my heart. Today, Reuben is an adult by standards of the state. He can go to war, buy cigarettes, rent dirty movies, and pay his own taxes. I don't see him buying cigarettes, but you can bet he'll be taking advantage of the movie rentals. When Faith appeared in a controversial magazine containing nudity, violence, and other forms of questionable substance, it was my darling baby-boy Reuben who couldn't be pulled away from the pages long enough to understand that his mother had just been fired from her job for the event! "That's stupid!" He announced as he continued pouring over the scantily dressed girls with pouting lips. "Sue the bastards!" he proclaimed while turning the book's pages slowly, staring at the third-world pictures exposing terrorism, violent scenes of massacre, public flogging, and a river of blood created by the death and destruction of thousands of dolphins illegally. I took his advice.

Every family needs a Laura Ashleigh. I have one. Laura is the older of my two Irish-twin daughters. She is 14 months older than my daughter Caity. Laura is forever and a day different from her sister in so many ways. She actually believes she was placed on Earth in order to control not only her own destiny but also that of every single person who comes into contact with her. For the most part she is fully capable of this responsibility, however, most of the time people resent being told what to do, when to do it, how to do it, and why they should be doing it. Luckily for me I am in desperate need of having someone exactly like my Laura Cakes to tell me what to do. Considering her sister Caity actually knows absolutely everything, it makes my life that much easier. All I have to do is wake up, think about living my own life, and put forth the slightest effort to do so. As soon as it has been detected that I am doing something so damning, Laura will come to my unwitting rescue with a daily agenda full of impossible tasks which carry more weight and critical need than I would have ever imagined. If for some reason I am unable to fulfill her every desire, need, want, or care, her sister Caity is quick to fill me in as to why she would never consider my actions wise. If these two girls didn't exist I might actually be forced to make a decision for myself. I would be left to the wolves when it came to planning my daily activities. I would never have the knowledge I do of Linkin Park lyrics, which member of Chemical Romance or Good Charlotte is going to be my new son-in-law, or how to do my makeup using predominantly dark circles around my already line-ridden eyes. Laura can care for a dozen, no, two dozen animals at one time, break horses that have never been ridden, sing songs which she has heard one time, correctly assemble a Sauder entertainment cabinet within an hour, but she can't make up her bed or remember to do the dishes. Amazingly, she has her little sister to scream at her from the back of the house—this is usually as effective as setting off lead balloons in the park, as you can imagine.

My last child, my youngest, is called many things, however I have taken to calling her Caity-Baby Baby-Caity ("CBBC") because she won't answer me if I were to call out her Christian given name of Caitlyn. There are some children (adults too) who do what they are going to do; I believe Dr. James Dobson had my precious CBBC in mind when he began his historical journey into the "Strong Willed Child". Where Caity may be only 15 years old, this powerhouse has lived the lives of many old women and then some. She has the knowledge and capabilities to not only be the smartest person ever, she is not the least bit shy about telling you that she will be Queen of America someday and that for this reason alone you should be careful when dealing with her. When God decided to make Caity He must have looked around Heaven, and noticed that one of the demons from Hell had been hiding out in the clouds where she could not be found easily. He must have gently disguised her as a tender, sweet cherub of a baby, making it virtually impossible to reject her. He couldn't decide which of his mischievous followers were deserving of her presence until the day he realized that I had never quite asked for full forgiveness for my own deeds as a child. Caity is quite literally the manifestation of the curse my mother placed on me when I was six years old; asking God and His Holy angels to grant me the privilege of raising a child exactly like myself. Not only do I love my baby Caity, I have to grin just a little when she thinks she has gotten away with yet another devious act. At times, I want to assist her in her paths knowing that I have already walked in her shoes . . . but alas, I let her fall, stumble, jump, and leap into her own world of experience; holding on tightly because of any and every consequence to follow. Would I give this child away? Some days yes, some days no, but if so, only to my mother, to remind her of what it could have been like if I had a twin!

It was Caity who had decided that a computer would be the answer to all of our problems, I think she was in the second grade when she made this proclamation. She convinced me to get a computer that would be capable of hooking up to the internet. At seven she had become capable of installing programs, running them, and even detecting if there were problems on the system. She wasn't savvy enough to understand the true manipulations of the machine before her, however, she was capable of logging on sites she wasn't suppose to be viewing. After a year or so of constant companionship with the keyboard she had successfully tapped into a few files belonging to United States Government agencies. It wasn't long before our doorbell rang and a man wearing dark glasses asked me for identification. He was serious when he asked to see my computer, and quite surprised when I explained that I really didn't know how to click out of one site to find another, let alone be able to hack my way into the Pentagon! While he stood in my living room staring at my complete inaptness, my mind was turning cartwheels over Caity. There she sat, on the floor watching Cartoon Network, oblivious to what mess she had created for her mom.

To be honest, I tell a little story which after it is told, anyone can understand the vast differences between my three children and their personalities. All families have this situation, it is nothing new, however, the clarification is often appreciated when it becomes necessary to clear Laura's name for something Caity has done by stealth, or that Reuben has blatantly blundered into. To compare Reuben to a Saint Bernard puppy makes more sense. He can be the biggest, sloppy-handed playmate, capable of leaping from the ground to the hood of the car in one bound; however, if that bound is misstepped he can be the 220 pound paper weight landing on your left arm, crushing it to pieces, which is exactly what he has done to me. "Hey Mom, watch this!" These words have trained me. I move immediately when I hear them, and usually behind a wall or some place safely out of his reach. To explain the differences of these three beautiful and most adored children, walk with me down a little parable.

It would seem that there is a barn in the middle of an open field. The barn is not in use, it hasn't been occupied for quite some time, but nevertheless, because the barn is not mine I am not inclined to do anything about it. My son Reuben comes to me in a state of excitement. He's all but leaping into the air because he has discovered a perfect 120-yard football field in which he can play. The only problem is, there is a barn sitting on top of the fifty-yard line. He wants to know where I keep the matches so that he can set the barn on fire and burn it to the ground. He offers no plan of operation really, just the plan of taking out the barn. There is no discussion of method, no explanation of consequence, my son has a one-track mind, and it works on one incredible event at a time. From time to time he is capable of miracles . . . but not today. "No Reu, you can't have the matches, burning barns that don't belong to us is wrong, and besides that, you could hurt yourself, your sisters, or someone else if the fire got out of hand." To my surprise, this answer is actually accepted and he walks away just as suddenly as he had entered the room. His mind racing on yet another plan all together different from the finding of a football field.

Within a few hours my peace is interrupted again. This time it is my daughter Laura. She has brought me lunch. She has created crackers with peanut butter, carrots, pieces of apples, and a freshly brewed cup of coffee just the way I like it, with a little creamer and a little sugar as well. She sits beside me and is actually about to feed me because Laura has it in her head that she is the nurturing member of the family. I thank her for her generosity but know there must be an explanation for the special treatment. Never one to lie, Laura takes a deep breath and pulls out a little fat notebook with reasons listed. She begins her request with a prelude of reasons why I should be listening to her completely. "Don't say anything Mommy, until I have finished. I know how you sometimes jump to the end, but this time just listen and hear what I have to ask." She continues her list of reasons why the barn in the middle of the field is a health hazard. She begins with the events that could possibly have happened to the people who either built the barn in the first place, or who had lived in the area when it was new. For a few minutes she has created the picture of horror that she believes will be impressive to me, as she brings me up to date with more current events, which could somehow take place if the barn were actually destroyed, and "carefully" removed. She is even quick to add that she has already called the various contractors of the area, and she has estimates of the cost. (I wondered who the men were out in the field this morning.) When she has finished she tells me that she is finished. She sits up pretty in her best smile and awaits my answer. Knowing that there is absolutely no way to be kind about it, I simply explain to her the governing practices of land leases, ownership, adverse possession under the state laws of Oklahoma, and how it could effect me as a bread-winner for the family if I give into her wishes. The last part about adverse possession intrigues her, and she is satisfied. It was merely a question in the first place, she explains. She goes to the door and yells out to her brother who is waiting on the field with a magnifying glass and shredded paper that she tried. Off she goes to align her horse collection in her room.

Before the night falls, I am welcomed by a smiling-faced little girl without front teeth. She seems docile, and yet the skin missing from her two knees would testify that she has been landing rather abruptly onto a hard surface. "You skinned your knees." I say to her as she climbs onto the cabinet and reaches to the top of the refrigerator for cookies I have placed out of her reach on purpose. Thump! Landing this time on her feet she makes a completely unintelligent statement regarding her injury. Swallowing her cookie somewhat she states clearly that it didn't hurt. The phone rings and it is just as I pick up the receiver that I am able to make out the silhouette of smoke, flames, fire fighters and trucks at the end of the field just outside my house.

"Hello", I say rather sheepishly into the phone. "Ma'am, do you have a little girl without front teeth? Is she wearing a blue t-shirt and a pair of green plaid shorts?" Someone is asking me. The caller ID identifies the call coming from the city police. "Someone saw her on top of the barn just before it went into its inferno. Seems she may have 'borrowed' a can of gasoline from a man down the way." I tell the kind officer that I have a daughter named Laura, she has been with me all day, in fact, she is not one to climb onto barns, and that I have a large boy named Reuben. He could have climbed onto the barn, yes, but if it was a little girl with missing teeth that he was looking for I couldn't possibly help him. As I hang up the phone I stop just short of picking up a long-handled axe from the closet door when I hear the sweetest little prayer coming from the girls' room. "Dear Jesus, Caity didn't mean to burn the barn. She wanted to make Reuben a football field for his birthday. She said she was sorry, and that tomorrow she'll get around to telling Mommy. Please let me do it God. I know how she is." With that, Laura's prayer for her baby sister ended and my ulcers began.

Where the story is not a true one, it clearly shows the vast differences between my three brats . . . kids, and it perhaps sets up the stories that are my life's treasure.

Chapter Two

Family. Erma Bombeck said they are the ties that bind . . . and gag. What truth lies in that statement. I wouldn't take another kid like any one of my own, and I wouldn't take a million dollars for any one of them either. Dealing with family is never easy, dealing with family requires having a faith in something, sometimes in everything. We've all heard it, it takes a village to raise a child. Well, it does. The church is a big part of that village, as is the school, teachers, neighbors, people on the street running away from my house, people calling me to inform me that they're missing a tool, a bike, a snake. I consider myself blessed and lucky to have been raised in a household where the faith we practiced was in Christ. It certainly couldn't have been Buddha that ruled over my brood, his beliefs don't allow fighting, clawing the eyes out of your siblings, standing on top of the chairs to get away from a flinging water balloon in the house, or ear-piercing screaming coming from the bathroom at the sight of wet bath towels draped over my open makeup which has been tipped over and is running freely onto the freshly mopped floor, and that's me! You should see how my kids live. Christ is all about forgiveness, Buddha never had my children; he never took a bath with a guinea pig or had to drive his daughter five miles to a toilet because she can't squat in the stables where she boards her horses, but she can go to school smelling like she's slept with them.

Where was Buddha when I found the catfish rotting in the back of my trunk that July afternoon? I didn't find him lurking in my closet the night I discovered my son's mushroom collection. He claimed it was a science project, but the black and purple painted hoods on the plants led me to believe he was up to something. The nicest thing about Reuben's insane mind is that when you ask him for a reason he doesn't always have one. He is completely satisfied with a helpless "I don't know why, it just looked good." If I tried to figure the boy out every time I ran across one of his imagination's feats I would spend a lifetime with a psychoanalyst. He simply can't be bothered with reason. Christ is big enough, strong enough, and wise enough for me to believe in Him. Every time I need something He has been there to at least provide strength to pull me through. I remember a specific incident during *one* of the ongoing custody battles that followed my divorce. I was sitting in the living room of a very small one bedroom apartment that I was renting. I had full custody of Reuben as he had been physically abused by my ex husband and had previously been awarded to me for this reason. The doorbell rang at 9:00 p.m. it was my daughter Laura. Always polite, she didn't know if it would be proper to simply walk into my apartment without asking. "Hello, come in. Did you walk?" I asked her. "Yes, Daddy said that if I wanted to see you I had to walk." The walk was about a mile, and even though it had not been incredibly dark at nine o'clock, I was devastated that he would have allowed an eight year old to make the trek. These are the moments when Christ has been most helpful. Laura needed $2.00 to go skating the next day at school. She told me she was the only one not going skating and that her dad was not going to give her the money because she had been a bad girl. When I asked her what she had done to make him feel that she was undeserving of the money or the privilege to go skating, her answer was a surprising "I told his wife that he had another girlfriend. I was only telling the truth Mom, it wasn't a lie and he knows it." I couldn't believe my ears. I couldn't believe what I was hearing.

Could it be true that this tiny figure of a girl had walked a mile to my house searching for the fare to skate the next day, and that she wasn't being given that opportunity by her father who wouldn't, or couldn't face up to the fact that he was hurting his own child by placing a greater value on his own philandering than he was in raising his daughter?

Why would she, at eight, even know about the affair? This hurt. I went to my purse, but as I did, I remembered that I had literally spent the last dollar I had on gasoline so that I could get to work the next day and be paid. If I didn't come up with the skating money Laura would never have blamed me, however, I knew it would be a sting in her heart if she were left behind while the rest of the class had fun. With a little faith in my heart, and 4 cans of Green Giant green beans in my cupboard, I took Laura down the road to the Wal-Mart store to exchange the cans for a couple of dollars. We entered the store just at the time that the customer service department was closing down. I looked at the hours of operation and realized that if something didn't happen now it would be too late for my daughter's situation. Walking up to the counter I asked Laura to sit on the bench provided for patrons that was just outside the ear range of the clerk named Maria that I needed to speak to. Explaining my situation to her was simple enough. I didn't expect the tears in her Hispanic brown eyes, but nevertheless, I welcomed them as I gave my daughter her skating money and used Wal-Mart's telephone to call her father to let him know she would not be going to his house that night. Maria took my hand and whispered into my ear that she had a good mother as well. She actually kissed my cheek and crossed herself. Being born a Baptist has never stopped me from accepting the faith of others if they are willing to pray for me. I considered this blessing a gift.

I think I hung up the phone before Laura's father could complain too much about the situation. More often than not he would be more upset about the fact that I found a way to appease the situation rather than to worry as to where his children are sleeping safely. Despite the manner of man her father is today, having been changed somewhat by time, at this particular time in my daughters' lives, he was not willing to sacrifice anything for them, nor was he willing to work with me with regards to making their lives any easier. I told him on the phone that I would appreciate it if he would bring Caity by my apartment, or allow me to pick her up, as the girls routinely slept in the same bed. It would be hard on Caity to be without her sister, and I couldn't bear to think of her crying herself to sleep. Naturally I was told no. I was told that I was not only *kidnapping* Laura, but that he would be calling the police to be sure they understood that I was refusing to return her. If I had pressed the issues the fight would have continued as it always did with him ranting about incompatible issues which had nothing to do with the situation whatsoever. He would finish his tantrum by threatening to physically harm Caity to prove that I was the one that was at fault. His methods of brutality would soon be shown in a court of law, but that day wasn't for several weeks away; or so I thought. I couldn't gamble with his insensitive mind. I had to let it go this time.

Sometime between dream one and dream two, as I held my tiny daughter in my arms, I could hear her snoring her way to a peaceful oblivion. Laura may be the most polite little girl in the world when she is awake, but that little red-head can wake the dead at night with her audibles. My only concern as I drifted back to sleep was for her sister. As I often do, I prayed quietly to God because I know He hears me. A simple "Be with Caity Baby" prayer was sufficient to ease my mind, as I know that God is fully in control, but nothing I could say or do at this minute could ease my heart. Mothers don't really sleep when their children aren't sleeping. Let me restate that; good mothers never sleep when their children aren't able to sleep.

Upon waking the next day I felt the unmistakable shock of being kicked in the head by the jerking foot of my youngest. I suppose sneaking out of her father's house, walking a mile in the middle of the night, using her key to enter the apartment and crawling into my bed without announcing herself, is just another way for her to let me know that no matter the circumstance Caity is fully capable of handling it. When things get hard for the rest of us Caity has an uncanny way of flipping the Devil off and going about things her own way. I swear sometimes I wonder if she doesn't have a brigade of battle-dressed angels hovering about her just in case she actually does step outside of bounds . . . again.

Faith in Christ is probably the only thing that has pulled me through the horrors that followed my divorce. The court records of Oklahoma county hold within their ancient walls the five inch folder numbered *FD97-4953; Stringfellow v. Stickley.* These are not the files from the first time I divorced Dale Stickley. However, they are the records of the final and most assuredly, the last time I divorced him. Prior to our divorce in 1997, Dale and I had decided that divorce would be the best solution for whatever one could call our relationship. I could stand here and place all the blame on his infidelity, his ranting, immature tyrant behavior, and gambling problems, but I'm sure there are more than enough books written about the trials and travails of a marriage united without good reason. I had problems too. I wouldn't allow his affairs. I refused to babysit his lover's kids, and that upset him.

Suffice it to say that because of what I deemed to be Christian morals, I decided to forgive his short comings and to marry him a second time following the very emotional event of the Oklahoma City Bombing. For Oklahomans, and for me in particular, having been downtown at the time of the bombing, making my way to the Alfred P. Murrah building when it exploded; I was living in a mental and emotional state of shock at that time, following the immediate event. I don't know what I was thinking, but it wasn't clear. Could this be a deeper sign from God that the divorce I was granted just six days ago was wrong? Perhaps I should be more forgiving, more understanding, or maybe I should have considered the fact that Reuben had already lost his biological father, and I was now taking him away from the man he had loved and trusted as a father for over nine years. Dale had been Reuben's baseball coach, his football coach, and his basketball coach at home. He had trained Reuben in martial arts and prayed with him at his bedside in 1993, when I had left the two of them alone in Texas while looking for a new home in Oklahoma.

Was I being selfish in not giving my marriage another try? Faith in God is one thing, letting emotions get in the way of making good judgments is entirely something else. Nearly every decision I have ever made about Dale was the wrong decision. I can't tell you why, but I know this: Heads and hearts do not come to the same conclusion, and where love is concerned, it would be best to listen to the head not the heart. The decision to remarry him was indeed the wrong decision. Within days of the Oklahoma City Bombing we were together again. Six days of being divorced had caused me to make an appointment with the Social Security office downtown to have my name changed on my Social Security card. The judge in that case had given me back my maiden name, even though in reality I had never wanted to change it to Stickley in the first place. One thing led to the other and I was forced to change my name when we purchased property together. Every time someone actually called me Jude Stickley I nearly cringed. It wasn't because I have an adverse reaction to Slavic surnames, it was basically because I had come to despise the last name of my husband when it was revealed to me that he wasn't even a Stickley. Talk about your Jerry Springer Shows, here's one for you. (Disclaimer: The details of this story vary depending on which member of Dale's family you talk to.) Dale's mother was born on the bayou of Mississippi, I don't think I was ever told much about her upbringing, only that she was out on her own making her own way by the age of twelve or thirteen. I do know that she met and married a man much older than she was, and that she gave birth to the first of her ten children by the time she was just over fourteen.

Whether she remained married to this man is a mystery, but what is known is that she continued "working" and "making her own way" for several more years. I was told by one of Dale's sisters that she married every father of every child, I find this fact hard to believe considering she herself couldn't tell me who Dale's father was, or who the father of her son that was born just before Dale was. She claimed this boy's father drove a taxi, and that Dale's father was a "shipyard dog". Her words were haunting of course, but fell on deaf ears when I tried to gather any truth from them by asking his sisters and brothers exactly what she meant by them. I was told that she was eight months pregnant with Dale when she married Mr. Stickley. Under Mississippi law, I was told, she had no other choice but to give Dale the last name when he was born.

Years into our marriage I became curious as to who Dale's father might actually be. With a little money and a private detective I discovered that his father's name was Bob Wilson, that he was a fisherman in Pascagoola, Mississippi, and that he wouldn't be interested in meeting his son or his two granddaughters. The cause was dropped, however not by every member of Dale's family. I continued to be harassed by his sisters, brothers, sisters-in-law, and others about the reasoning behind my investigation. I suppose I would have to admit that the knowledge of who my husband's real family was could be beneficial to my daughters if they were ever to engage in a study of genealogy, however, I was actually more driven by the fact that his mother's choice of men to raise her family and to take care of her was less than desirable. When Dale's youngest sister was only twelve years old Dale began petitioning me to help him gain legal guardianship of her, claiming that every other sister had been physically abused. Dale claimed also that he had been assaulted by his father when he was around the age of nine, having denied these claims since our divorce; nevertheless, we engaged in an open attempt at trying to get full and legal custody of his sister. Their 'father', it turns out was an adopted child himself. He is not truly a born Stickley. The name had absolutely no worth to me as Dale's wife, and I could think of no better name to claim than that which was given to me at my birth, the name of my own father, Stringfellow. Stringfellow is the name I returned to my son, and to Laura as well. Caity remains a Stickley.

It's never easy going through the files that collect dust at the court house and forever remind you of the great mistakes you have made throughout the years, but having changed my name back to Stringfellow was something I never regretted. The change would not come as easily as I had hoped the day I parked my car at the Myriad Convention Center and walked up Robinson toward the Murrah building. When the explosion came I was knocked to the ground forcibly with the strangest sensation I could ever imagine. It was as if my ears were turned off, and my eyes were somehow positioned all over my head. I saw paper flying, smoke rising, blood on the concrete beneath my knees, and people running. I can't remember standing up and I certainly don't remember talking to anyone. I remember thinking that a gas main had exploded and for whatever reason I believed it was on Robinson. I crossed the street at Dean McGee and ran easterly to the next main street, it was called Broadway. The Myriad Convention Center was at the end of the street and I clearly remember not being able to run quickly to my car. It was as if I was dreaming that I was running and my legs were stone. They wouldn't move, I had to push them with my hands and make them go. When I reached the car I was being helped by a man in a business suit that wanted to know what had happened. I don't know, I told him. I don't know. I was driving my father's little truck downtown that day because I had a couple of interviews with the Medallion Hotel. One of my appointments was for 10:00 a.m. and one was for 3:00 p.m.

I couldn't start my truck without keys and I couldn't find my keys. My hands wouldn't lift themselves up to help me, and I remember staring at my purse where I'm sure the keys were laying at the bottom waiting to be engaged. It must have only been a few minutes, but for that time I felt no time at all. My ears were still ringing from what must have been the enormous blast. Finally, with my keys in place and my truck pulling out I reached for the radio to hear a little music. Perhaps that would help somehow. I could get out of downtown, call the hotel to let them know I would not be coming to the interview, when the thought occurred to me that the gas main could be taking out the hotel as I driving past it. The Medallion was also on Robinson. I remember going an entirely different way home than what I am used to in order to avoid the downtown area. It wasn't for several minutes that I realized that the truck I was driving didn't have a radio. The noises I was hearing and the sounds of the day weren't music being played at all. Sirens, multiple sirens were echoing off of one another. Hundreds of police, EMT, fire truck sirens, rescue squads, and bells from everywhere were mixing in the air into a crescendo of noise making it virtually impossible to think of anything other than disaster. I do remember driving away and looking into the sky just above the area that the Murrah building would have been located; thick heavy smoke raced into the air, but with it I could see a white line of what appeared to be a streamer, or a cutting edge going through the smoke. Months later I read where people had claimed to have seen angels directly above the building. I wish now that this would have been my vision, but I can honestly say that I didn't sense any peace at that moment. I knew in my heart that God was aware of what had happened, yes, but this comfort was because of faith, not the application of that belief. Not at that minute.

Immediately following the bombing I drove my father's truck back to his house. No one was home. I sat in my parents' living room out in the country on a little farm located about 25 miles northeast of the blasted area from downtown. The time it took to drive to their house was enough time for news coverage to begin explaining what would turn out to be the nation's worst terrorist act on American soil until the events of 9/11. Until April 19, 1995, no Americans had been killed by terrorist on American soil. The immediate response to the day's happenings were somewhat predictable. Terrorists from the Middle East were being blamed for what had taken place. My name change would be the least of my concerns as I began attempting to contact my three children who were in school and daycare at the time. Phone lines were jammed. Hours would pass before my parents came home, and even more hours would pass before I was able to drive to pick up my children from school, as the schools were not allowing children to be released until more information could be given to them. With little else to do I decided to go to the local hospitals to see if I could help. This was a mistake as they were inundated with people who were professionally trained to assist. I thought about giving blood and would have except I was actually losing it from my knees and elbows. I wondered if anyone would take mine—it would be the first time in my life that I had ever volunteered to give my own blood.

When people ask me why I married my husband after I had divorced him in 1995, I usually come back with the standard, boring answer of "I felt it was my Christian obligation to forgive him for his infidelity. He said he was sorry, and we needed to be married for the children." The real reason is much more simple. I was incredibly stupid. If I have one regret it would be remarrying a man I knew I couldn't trust. Forgiving him for sleeping around on me didn't mean I had to give him another shot at me. I literally put myself and my family back into a bad situation, a berth of events for many more years to come because I couldn't get over myself. If I had the least bit of Christian education at the time I was reconciling with my ex, I would have realized that the angels flapping their wings in front of me were warning signs, not applause! Leave it to me to think the best thing to do to patch up a bad marriage is to give it another chance with the same two idiots in the starring roles. It didn't take long before we weren't going to church again, we weren't paying bills again, and we weren't living in a nice house again. Again, after the bombing and just before the next time we moved, we were living with my parents, an event that seemed to be taking place on the average of once a year since 1988, when I married the man in the first place. I can count the times I moved on two hands, but unfortunately I can also count the years that passed between these moves on one. My son had attended three first grade classes in three different schools in two different states, because my husband's job had moved us around. My mother took to writing my addresses and phone numbers in pencil, and my friends stopped asking if they could help me move. They knew I would be taking them up on it. I don't think my best friend

Jeannie, who I have known since my first day in high school has even seen seven of the houses I lived in from the day I was married to the day I divorced . . . the first time.

To his credit, (and I don't say that often) my ex husband wasn't completely to blame for the moves. He worked for American Airlines for a while, and for several different loan companies which were up and coming in the early nineties. They moved us back and forth from Oklahoma City to Tulsa on several occasions. At one point we weren't even sure which storage center held our furniture. Our move from the only permanent house we actually owned had nothing to do with Dale, and everything to do with Caity Baby becoming so sick from asthma and what the doctors thought could have been cystic fibrosis. On the night of April 1, 1993, Caity became so ill that I could hardly get her to the emergency room in time. Of course, there were no doctors on call at the hour of the night that I brought the baby into the hospital, and just like you see now on television, I was screaming as I went through doors of the emergency rooms calling out for help. When a doctor was called and a nurse was summoned to start the ventilator I finally realized that Caity was turning blue from lack of oxygen. She would breathe. I don't know if it was instinct or a mother's mechanics, but I thumped the kid in the back with a considerable amount of force. The blow either upset her to the point that she wanted to wail at me, or it was exactly what she needed. Caity began breathing, and took the next twelve minutes of her life to shriek into my ear, alternating the oxygen mask between breaths, tears flying out of her two eyes, hands pulling out my hair, and legs kicking me in the privates as she thought about what she was being subjected to. It was the most wonderful moment as I realized my baby wasn't blue anymore, she was fully capable of perpetrating extreme pain to my groin, all the while puncturing my eardrums with her tantrums. I had to thank God, I had to praise Him right then and there for her nasty little I-will-not-die-you-can't-make-me attitude. It wasn't a week later that our house was sold, and we were moving to Midland, Texas so that my baby girl could have a fighting chance at gaining weight, size and the true ability to breathe on her own. I swear to God (and yes, I do that a lot) if He had given asthma to Laura instead of Caity I would have been interrupted in my sleep with a simple little wheeze and an apology. "Mother, I'm sorry . . . I'm such a . . . bother. I don't . . . . mean . . . . to . . . . die, but could . . . . you take . . . . me . . . . to the . . . . doctor.? Please . . . . and thank . . . you."

Not that Laura hasn't had her emergency room adventures. Wow . . . now that I'm writing this I realize that my children have nearly died more than a dozen times or more from whatever events take place in these uncertain times. Looking back at the memories that come to mind I think of the day I caught Laura and Caity doing cartwheels on a 4" beam-type railing that my dad had constructed around his house in the country. The house is actually a trailer that he has built any number of decks and porches around. At some points the decks are nine feet off the ground, at others they are only 4 feet from Terra Firma. You don't have to guess which end of the house the girls were turning flips on. It's rather like the day my dog realized he couldn't run along the top of the fence as he chased the birds and found himself on the other side of the fence facing the neighbor's rottweiler. I would have given anything to have recorded his facial expression at that encounter. But I digress.

Back to the emergency room adventure with Laura. We were living in Moore, Oklahoma, a sleepy little community nestled between Oklahoma City and the University of Oklahoma in Norman. Being a working mom, I had the responsibilities of picking up the kids, getting the groceries, paying the bills, making dinner, and cleaning the house before the kids were put to bed. Dale worked nights and was unable to do much of the daily chores which somehow were pushed onto me even though I worked as a legal secretary and had a part time job selling insurance. It was sometime in February, I know there was snow on the ground, as I pushed the garage door opener, drove my 1992 White Mazda Protégé into the garage and told the kids to sit still while I unloaded the groceries.

I would only be a minute, I put Reuben in charge. That wasn't the most intelligent decision, as he was not quite six at the time. Nevertheless, both the girls were in their car seats in the back of the car, the groceries were in the trunk, and as was my habit, I had left the garage door leading to the house open so the cat could do her business in the cat box located in the garage. If things had gone to plan I would have been back in 30 seconds, the groceries set on the counter or in the frig in the sacks, where I could deal with them later . . . that didn't happen.

Laura, who couldn't bear to be without her mother for more than 10 seconds began climbing out of her car seat. She was only two and a half years old, but fully aware of the mechanical workings of the buckle strapped across her chest. With the front door of my car open so that I could make easy access back to my family, Laura crawled out of the back seat, over the front seat, fell out of the car completely, and raised her tiny head off the ground where she had smacked it. The front door design of the 1992 Mazda Protégé, I soon realized, were made in such a way that the door comes to a severe point. This severe point met my daughter's forehead as she lifted her tearful, screaming face off the garage floor. My son left the car shouting at me, trying to tell me that Laura got out of her car seat. I couldn't see her because she was literally on the ground in a dark garage, with her head completely attached to the bottom of the door of my car. When I did manage to find her I was immediately struck with the impossible task of getting her head unstuck. They don't teach you these things in college . . . . there is no manual wherein you can look up this sort of need in a section marked *"Troubleshooting when your child's head must be removed from the edge of your car door"*. Without blinking, I placed my right foot on top of Laura's head and pushed her head off the car door. In one swift move I picked Laura up, opened the passenger door, and swung her back into her car seat. I called out to Reuben, telling him to go next door to get the neighbor to watch him and Caity. Reuben was already getting Caity out of her car seat. I remember driving off with the back of the trunk open because I had not closed it after getting my groceries out.

This was during the days of big, fat, heavy, car phones. The neighbor I asked Reuben to run to wasn't home. I could see this as I drove past her house to the nearest hospital. I called another neighbor whose number was on speed dial. I quickly explained my situation to her, and like an angel Lori Weeks came to my rescue. She lived next door and was so down to earth and sweet I knew she would be able to handle the children in a crisis. Just as before, there were no doctors on call at the little hospital, and I found myself calling out for help the second I came into the emergency room. Laura, unlike my blue baby Caity, was not quiet. The Republic of China could have heard her crying and calling out "No, No!" as I fought time and what I assumed death, to find someone with a medical degree. Within a few minutes I had convinced the E.R. assistant that I was not about to take time to answer her questions at this time. I would answer them as my child received medical attention, yes, I did have insurance, I would be giving her the card just as soon as I could, but that if she didn't do something at this very second, I would be bringing down the Health Department, my attorney, and every professional I could find to close the hospital down immediately for putting my child in further danger. I think she believed my tyrant behavior. It was either that, or the look in my crazed eyes as I demanded attention for my baby. It has never ceased to amaze me how a small town hospital with a limited staff can assume that there will not be an emergency on any given day at any given minute. When life and death swing in the balance, please people, hire the staff necessary to perform whatever is necessary. I realize our health insurance capabilities in this country could be better, but to under staff intentionally is begging for law suits.

Laura's head had not bled. This was not a good sign to the doctor. He realized that the wound had to be deep if I were telling him the truth about how I had managed to get her off the edge of the front door of my car. He looked at me, asked me to hold her tightly, as he took a long pair of a tweezer looking instrument and gently pulled the inverted flap of baby skin on my daughter's forehead, just above her right eyebrow. Upon doing this, an immediate gush of red blood spurted forth out of her head, causing she and I both to scream with fright. I screamed because it hit me in the face, she screamed from either the pain, or the shock of seeing that much blood coming out her own face. Though they tell us that head injuries bleed worse, and that most of the time these sort of injuries look worse than what they are, Laura and I were both rather put into shock from the blood flowing all over the emergency room floor. The nurse assigned to help the doctor was not only equipped at handling the noise coming from my child, she managed to give me clear directions as to how to hold Laura for the suturing procedure. Six tiny stitches were required on the outside of the wound, eight on the inside. I couldn't believe the way her tiny chest expanded and released during each knot. It was as if she was telling the world that she was being killed and I was helping the people hold her down to do it. I cried like I had never cried before, but even through this moment of pain, hurt, torture, and healing, I remember whispering to Jesus for help. I remember whispering to Jesus to be with the doctor, to be with the baby, to be with me . . . . I cried again as the nurse reached past my body, which was literally laying on Laura to hold her in place, as she stated out loud that *Jesus* was a welcomed name in the E.R. I left the hospital feeling the power of God, and knowing that even though bad things happen to good people, I am absolutely never alone. I don't have to think I am, I don't have to fear that I will ever be left out in the cold without a way to escape hard times. Having just a *little faith* is better than having a great deal of hope.

Sometimes having a family can be challenging in other ways. I don't know how it happens, or why it happens, but my children and I never have been on the same time table. When they're born they wake up when they want to, forcing me to feed them. People told me to put them on my schedule . . . right! You do it. You come over to my house, and you tell this wiggling, screaming, take-no-prisoners brat to shut up, go to sleep and get over himself. You come over to my house at 2:43 a.m. on a Tuesday, when I have to get out of bed at 6:00 a.m., and you tell the little tyke that she will be given a bottle when it's time to give her one. Diapers can wait, feedings can wait, train the kid to do what he or she is suppose to do, that way you can rest and the entire parenting experience can be a rewarding one. Let me know the success rate on that one. Maybe I can get a grant to study the likelihood of that happening any time soon.

Chapter Three

It's time to introduce my other family, the one I started out with. Stone Mountain, Georgia. Dad, Mom, two sisters, a brother and me, 1972.

Journal entry: (revised)

"We left Grandpa with the animals, he can handle it, what was he by now? 81? If I was born when he was 71, and I'm 10 now . . . then yes, he must be yes, 81. Wow . . . he's getting old. It was just last year that he was only 80 and getting into the lake with me. He only has one leg, the doctor took off the other one and he has a big heavy wooden leg with his shoe attached to it. We went swimming and he just stood there. Then he got out of the water, but when he did he fell into it and his leg popped off. It's not like it hurt or anything, he was laughing, but his leg was floating out to the buoy. (I think you spell it that way). I had to go get it and since it had a strap on it, I just put it in my mouth and paddled back. That was hard.

There was a lady with her kid on the beach laughing at me but that's OK, Grandpa needed to laugh after that. I think it's funny because on Sunday I saw him dusting his foot off. It was just something that struck me as being funny that's all. We left him with the animals; Rover, and Lady Wayne, our dogs, and he can feed them and make sure the mail gets brought in. Our mail box is too small for three days worth of stuff. I think about that and I don't know why. We're going camping again, but this time we're going to Stone Mountain, Georgia, all the way to the other side of the country. I'm in the back again, but I don't care. I'll sleep."

Three weeks of camping and the thing is, we didn't realize that our 14 foot Shasta trailer was in stark contrast to everyone else's nice big trailers. I guess Mom realized it, but we kids didn't know. We knew we had to walk the block to the bathhouse to use the toilets and showers, and we knew that Dad and my brother Mike had to sleep in the back of the truck because there were only three beds in the trailer and four girls. We knew that we had to use a cooler instead of a real refrigerator, but that thing was always full to the hilt with orange and grape *CRUSH*. There's no way we cared about silly things like bigger and better living facilities. What do kids know? We swam in the lake and laid on the white beach, totally ignoring the fact that a chain gang wearing striped pajamas and who were shackled to one another were literally building that beach truck load by truck load. The authorities told us to stay away from the prisoners, they told us that they couldn't talk to us, but these men were really very friendly. One even told me I was pretty and that I reminded him of his own little girl Lily. Lily, that's a pretty name. I didn't tell him my name, and it was partly because I wasn't sure of it. I was just then at that time in my life beginning to play with the name I wanted to be called. My dad had always called me JUDE and my mother called me JUDY. My brother called me Boot, which came out of a name game of Judy Booty. My teachers called me other things when they thought I wasn't listening, but I was always listening. Just because I didn't show up to school and sit in their class didn't mean I wasn't there! I usually could be found. I liked my little hiding places around Apollo Elementary. I was in the fourth grade and fourth graders hide a lot.

It was about the same time, maybe a year before, that I had decided not to match my socks anymore, and this particular summer was a perfect time to make sure on my promise to my mother who told me that if I wasn't going to actually match my socks and put them in the drawers where they belonged, she had better never see me wearing them matched ever again. FINE! I wouldn't match my socks and she couldn't make me. I would unmatch them in fact. I didn't know my name necessarily, and I liked it better when my Grandpa called me Pumpkin anyway. Sometimes

I thought about the mail box being too small to hold a pumpkin and sometimes I thought about putting socks in it just to surprise my mom. I liked 1972, the music was awesome. I remember being in love with so many different singers and bands. My favorite of course, was (and still is) the Bee Gees. I had a few of their records and even an album called Cucumber Castle, but one of the Brothers Gibb, Robin, wasn't on it. It didn't matter, Maurice was, and he was really the cutest anyway. He had to be a little shorter than Barry was, but he looked much better in tights. He had a dog too, in the pictures, and there was even a song about dogs on the album. I loved dogs. I loved Maurice, I loved the Beatles, I loved Elvis. I think mostly I loved looking in the fan magazines and seeing more boys than I even knew could be singers. Neil Young was good too, my sister had his records, but he wasn't cute.

My sister Linda was in love with Bobby Sherman and David Cassidy. She told me I couldn't love them so I didn't. It didn't matter because I was going to marry Maurice. He was English. That was until 1977, when I decided I was going to marry Derek Longmuir of the Bay City Rollers. He was blond too, and he played the drums. He was Scottish, so I decided that my last name was Scottish. I told everyone it was, but in the real world I knew it was English.

My friend Robin (not the member of the Bee Gees) was my age and we used to walk our dogs together. We had been really close bestest friends since before kindergarten because my dad worked with her mom and my mom watched her. She didn't need babysitting because she wasn't a baby. She told me so, and I believed her. I was the same age and I didn't need a babysitter either. Robin loved Derek too and we were both going to marry him. I told her she could have him half the week and I could have him the other half. This didn't seem to bother her so the deal was struck. Besides being in love with the same musicians Robin was a musician herself. She could play the piano and she didn't even need sheet music in front of her. I used to sit on the stairs in her house and pretend to be in a mansion. Her house, a ranch style two story house, was a mansion compared to mine, but nevertheless, I used to sit on the stairs and pretend that I was in the moors of England in my mansion and Derek didn't mind being in England instead of Scotland because he had been living in Scotland all of his life. We could live happily anywhere and Robin liked England too. This fantasy was a good one.

In 1978, just a mere 18 months from the time I had decided to marry Derek and share him with my bestest friend, I had become much more mature about relationships. I was no longer going to marry the drummer of the Bay City Rollers because I was in love with a real guy who lived in the same city that I did. I was going to marry him instead. He went to my school and he was tall, blond, and played football. Football, it would seem, took up more of my time than anything else at this point. I found myself sitting on the bleacher seats outside during practice. It didn't matter if it was raining, snowing, hot as hell, or just perfect enough to fly a kite. I watched the boys play ball. I wanted to understand the game completely so that I could impress my new conquest. He and I would have football babies and we'd go off into the world together with or without Robin. In fact, it was going to have to be without Robin, or as she also had changed the spelling of her name, and was now being called Robyn, because her circles had not included me for quite some time. My new best friend was Jeannie Larwig, two grades higher than me in school, but she didn't have any problem with me wanting to graduate a year early, or with my new obsession with "Blondie" or football. She even came over to watch it on television with me from time to time. Jeannie couldn't make up her mind which of the Bay City Rollers she liked but she was dead set on being in love with Barry Gibb. Barry was the oldest Gibb of the Bee Gees and that was fine with me since I was still secretly in love with Maurice. I did find his marriage to Yvonne somewhat annoying, but after all, he hadn't met me before he proposed marriage to her, so I suppose all is fair when something like that happens. That, and the fact that he was nearly 12 years older than me, a famous rock star, and that we had never met.

Jeannie had a real stereo and it even had an 8-track cassette player, something my one armed record player didn't. By this time I had acquired quite a few 8-tracks including the Bee Gees' Mr. Natural, which had another song about dogs on it, and Jeannie liked dogs as much as I did. Jeannie, like Robin, had been born into a family with just a tad more money than my own. I lie of course, she was the daughter of a very affluent family on both her mother and her father's side, but to look at how she dressed, carried on, and even talked, you wouldn't have known she was anything other than normal . . . poor like me. We hit it off the first minute we saw each other because we had so many things in common; boys, football, and the Bee Gees. And doughnuts.

It was Jeannie who went to the Bee Gees concert with me in 1979, when I saw and met Maurice for the first time. Infact, it was Jeannie, and still is Jeannie, who I call my best friend. She and I have been to many concerts and events together, but the highlight of our years as friends had to be the August 4, 1979 Bee Gee concert in Oklahoma City. Neither she nor I can remember what led up to the moment really, but both remember the second the two of us spotted one another in the hotel lobby or foyer. Strangely, I recall the first glance as if it was happening still. I hadn't been such a fan that I was going out of my way to go up to their room; however we were staying in the same hotel on the floor below the Bee Gees and their people. As I was coming back from checking a message at the front desk Jeannie called my attention to the fact that the Bee Gees, or at least Robin and Maurice, were walking through the lobby on their way to the elevator. She called out my name and Maurice answered her. He said "What?" as if she had called him instead. For a second we stood about four feet from one another and stared at each other without a single word. Robin was trying to get Maurice's attention because the elevator (the lift as he called it) had arrived. Robin had not wanted to ride the elevator, saying he preferred the stairs, but they were staying on the 10th floor. No one really paid the least bit of attention to what Robin was saying except for Jeannie, who related the one-sided conversation to me later. Robin ended up taking the elevator up, not waiting on Maurice, who had been so distracted that he hadn't moved. I couldn't explain the feeling exactly, and I can't tell you now what it was that was happening, but it has been a source of reoccurring peace in my mind every time I think about it. We both sort of half smiled and he said to no one in particular, "Oh, I'm sorry, I thought you were talking to me." Jeannie nodded toward me as if to say, No, I was talking to my best friend. Putting out my right hand I shook Maurice's, and without talking we just stood there. No one else was there. Nothing was around us, it was as if the air was missing as well, but I didn't care. He couldn't stop looking at me, and I was not about to stop staring back at him. "I know you." He said.

"I know. I know you too." I replied

"No," he continued, "I mean, I think I know you. We've met before. A very long time before now. I don't know when." He questioned himself.

"I know, it was before—" and I stopped suddenly. I couldn't believe the words were about to come out of my mouth. I wasn't necessarily into the metaphysical in 1979.

"Are you coming to the concert?" he asked.

"Yes, we've got floor seats. We're staying on the 9th floor by the way. Room 906."

"Come to my side of the stage when the show starts. I'll tell Steve to let you stand there. I have to go." And with that, he was leaving.

"Jude. My name is Jude."

"I know. I don't know how I know that, but I know." His elevator returned and he never stopped smiling and as the doors shut he was shaking his head as if to clear a cobweb.

Those words took me to the moon instantly. Nothing sexual. Nothing out of the extreme, just a meeting of someone who thought perhaps we had been friends in another time. I wasn't into that sort of thinking at the time. Today I know more about when we met for the first time and Maurice had been right. It was many years before that concert encounter. My faith at the time of our meeting was embedded in what I call the Baptist Box. It is a safety net really, a place where I had been trained, conditioned, and held in complete harmlessness. The only problem with the Baptist Box is that it would not allow outside thinking. My heart was hurting, pounding in fact, my head trying to reach beyond that which I was accustomed to, but to no avail. I couldn't release the seams of that box. I didn't realize it at the time, but over time I would have to squeeze out of the box entirely if I had any hope of living by faith. I read a quote recently by Robin Gibb, Maurice's fabulous twin brother. He stated that he didn't see why he couldn't pretend, or think of Maurice as being alive still in this world, if people were saying that people existed in other worlds after they had passed away. Like Robin, I can't see or think of Maurice as being dead. He isn't dead. He did die, but only for a second or two really. After his passing, he came right back to us. To anyone that is who is willing to let him in. I don't pretend that Mo is alive, he is alive. What are the options? No, really, what would the options be if we didn't have faith? Why would preachers, priests, those we love, and family or friends SAY that someone is in another place if they didn't think it true? This faith is different from what we're taught in Sunday School, I understand that, but in the past few years since his passing, I have seen, felt, heard, sang with, danced with, loved, and been loved by Maurice Ernest Gibb in a very sweet and kind manner. I can't say why, how, or much more about it, but the smile on my face is real, and the pain in my heart gone. He is alive. Robin . . . he is alive, and he is here. I love your faith, and it helps. It really helps to know that faith is universal, deep, different, shared, and accepted in so many forms.

It wouldn't be right to not mention an incredible legacy left by Mo through his beautiful daughter Samantha and her band MEG. MEG, of course stands for *Maurice Ernest Gibb*, and has been performing for quite a few years under a couple of names in Miami. MEG has recently released their first major CD titled simply *MEG the Samantha Gibb Project*. You have to listen to it; Sam's voice creates a medley of field and flowers against a backdrop of youth and experiences that only the daughter of a very talented music man can produce. I think of Amy Lee from *Evanessence*. Maurice's son Adam also provides additional lyrics, some written with Lazaro Rodriguez, Samantha's longtime boyfriend and the band's technical and guitar lead. Maurice actually produced most of the songs on the CD, perhaps the best way in my opinion to keep his heart alive. MEG consists of Nik Sallons on Bass, Brando Garcia on guitar, Kris Morro on drums and the silent man, sound genius simply known on the *www.megmusic.net* website as "Gabe". You guys are awesome! Keep the music burning!

Chapter Four

Flash forward—30 years. Family: for me it is myself, my son, a football playing, football eating, football breathing, football pooping boy with nothing on his mind other than the strategies, tasks, challenges, statistics and schedules of the game. Where Reuben is not the son of the boy I was in love with in High School, he certainly could have been when you consider the vast connection he has to the gridiron. There is Laura, my docile, sweet-natured daughter who takes in every stray animal she finds, even if she must convince it to follow her home in order to become an official stray, and there is my younger daughter Caity, who, as before mentioned, is a demon posing as a little girl. Wouldn't you have loved to have seen the look on Satan's face the day Caity took Christ into her heart? Not that any of us ever doubted that it would happen in the first place, but to be quite honest, she has been what some would call an unorthodox Christian. For Caity there was never the restraint of the Baptist

Box. She had managed to live within the confines of an invisible boundary which simulated the Box, but thank goodness, it was *"more or less a guideline"*; to steal a phrase from Captain Barbosa! Even her baptism was somewhat of a fluke. We happened to be at a creek one day in the early spring of 1999, when Caity announced that she was ready to be baptized. The only suitable person handy was my friend Nancy Henry, who's credentials included being a Christian, a flower-child, and the daughter of a Baptist preacher. Her father had passed away, but she was sure he would be able to guide her through the event. Cold as the water was, my little girl got into it, stood freezing her butt off as she was completely immersed and as she was *"raised to walk in forgiveness of Christ"* by my good friend, the clouds began to break and God gave us a little smile through a ray of sun. It was official. Family: I'll keep mine. Usually people would say that I don't find it the least bit difficult to talk about myself. Perhaps writing for prosperity may prove to be a different experience for me. I can tell you that I am a well educated woman, this much cannot change from one person's opinion of me to the other. I hold a PhD in Administration, and a Masters degree in Literature from Oklahoma City University, a private college in the heart of the capital city where tuition can run as much as ten times higher than the state colleges, however, due to its proximity to my office at the time I was attending college, Oklahoma City University was an easy choice to make. I could literally run to work a few minutes late having completed a class, go on my lunch hour for another class three days a week, and pick up a night class as well. Oklahoma City University doesn't offer any doctorate programs other than Law, and where I was fully capable of attending, the judge in my family court case made it perfectly clear to me that if I were to pursue a degree in Law I would be doing so without my children. Before you go off thinking that the judge doesn't have that much power, I need to remind you that I not only agree with you, I made my point in court, which cost me several months of custodial rights as well as my standing with the good judge. It wasn't until I was able to hire the junkyard dog of an attorney that I ended up with, that I was able to make the slightest bit of sense of the laws as they were interpreted by the judge in my case. It seemed to me as if she made up the rules as she went along, and while she was doing that, she decided that I wasn't necessarily important enough to be in the courtroom when she handed down her judgments against me. Obviously, truth was completely out of the question, it all boiled down to what my attorney knew that my ex's attorney didn't know, what my attorney could use as leverage over the judge, and how far she was willing to use her wisdom of the laws in court without blackballing herself for any future cases. I just knew that at any given moment the two red-headed bitches, my attorney and the judge, would be going at each other with case law flying, decisions being challenged, and compromises being reached, all without my knowledge of what I was agreeing to; without Anita Sanders standing in as counsel, I can say now that I would not only have lost custody permanently, I would probably have been hauled away to the pokey for suggesting that the judge in my case actually go by the big, fat, statutory law books upstairs from her office located in the Law Library of the courthouse. I was quite sure I could have found at the very least three or so laws she had arbitrarily decided needed her personal touch before administrating them to me and to my family.

As I was saying, Oklahoma City University didn't offer a doctorate program, and I know enough to know that if I wanted to teach at the college level full time I would need at least one post graduate degree in whatever discipline it was that I wanted to teach. On line universities seemed to be the only option left, with a Ph.D. In Administration, I remain to this day, an educator. That is not to say that I am paid well, in Oklahoma the words *"Education"* and *"Money"* seldom go hand in hand. More appropriately, the words *"Education"* and *"Adjunct"* go well, or *"Education"* and *"Unemployed"* go steady quite often as well.

Admittedly, I am a self-proclaimed arguer. It's not necessarily that I think the entire world would be better off if I were in charge, it's just that I think it would be a great idea to at least let me give it a good try at some level. I'm quite capable (on paper anyway) to run a university or community college. According to my resume I've taught at, written for, researched, and been employed by several colleges and/or universities. Adjunct here, adjunct there, here an adjunct, there an adjunct, everywhere an adjunct. Do I seem bitter to you? I drove 86 miles a day to work three days a week, and 44 miles a day two days a week, for longer than I care to remember. Working for three separate colleges, teaching three entirely different types of students every semester, keeping my books, bags, papers, and supplies in the back of my already overcrowded trunk, trying to convince the administrations of each facility to hire me full time. It was always the same answer, no money in the budget. No money this semester, no money in the future, not unless we get another endowment. It was unlikely that any of the crusty old dogs on campus were going to die any time soon. Students had been secretly praying for that miracle without me even suggesting it. Chapel at one of the colleges I worked at could certainly be a lively event when the students decided to actually wake up and be counted. I remember a girl praying that she got her period! Needless to say, she was asked not to return the following semester. I was asked to fail her if I could. Such is the way of life at a private Christian based university in the Bible

Belt of America. Being a Christian myself didn't eliminate me from the claws of the traditionally minded gargoyles sitting in their oak chairs above the mossy walls of the old rigid school. I made the mistake of wearing a Viking helmet on October 31, declaring the day to be a wonderful day to study pagan rituals as a means of understanding the differences in the various religions students would be faced with once they graduated and left the hallowed grounds of the sacred campus. Needless to say, I was not asked to return the next semester! Such is the way of life at a private Christian based university in the Bible Belt of America.

If my faith wasn't tested during my failing marriage, as I tried to struggle with the questions of whether or not to forgive my husband's philandering, it was certainly tested as I applied for jobs in the state of Oklahoma under the impression that an education and experience were all that is necessary to be hired full time at a state or private university in the capacity of an English Professor. How wrong I was; how could I have known that being able to work 18 hours rather than the national average of 12 is required. How could I possibly compete with candidates who are married to staff members, administrators, legislative members, and those who are employed by the state of Oklahoma? If the world was somehow suppose to be fair in its dealing I wasn't made aware of it. Semester after semester I drove from one far reaching county to the next, adjunct teaching and teaching two or three classes a day for less than what could be considered decent pay, without benefits, and without the respect given to full time faculty. Certainly I deserve to be hired, if experience and education mean anything. Until then, I'll write.

Chapter Five

Faith is a strange and unique choice we make, something we intentionally intend to do. It isn't fate or what may happen. It is, if you can understand it, the actual force behind the reason we believe something will or must happen. I use the word choice because it isn't an emotion. It isn't something that you take lightly, use without consideration, or put up on a shelf to take down during the ravages of a storm or tornado. That would be the word *"prayer."* According to the author of Hebrews (who is that anyway?) Faith is the substance of things hoped for, the evidence of things unseen. Faith completes my prayer life as I conclude with the words "In Jesus' name", without the evoking of the name itself there is no hope for an answer to whatever the petition may be. *Faith* is the reason we look for the sun to come up in the morning, not hope. We already know there is a promise given that there will be another tomorrow. Believing it, living your life as if you know it will happen, that's faith. By faith I was able to face the judge over and over again, even though in times past she had continuously made monumental statutory errors in her rulings. There was always something inside of me that said "She can't do that, you can get another attorney, you can prove to her and to everyone else willing to listen that she's not legally allowed to take these actions against you. Keep the faith, keep the faith, keep the faith." I remember the day my wicked and wretched judge leaned up out of her chair when I had corrected her, this was before I had proper representation, but at a time when it was obviously clear that the law was on my side. She leaned up out of her chair on the platform, shook her face and hand at me and demanded of me as to whether or not I was an attorney! She repeated herself twice, and I was hoping to find her threats being recorded, only to find out that her clerk was not required to record everything that happened in her courtroom; only those things during which time the judge was controlling what was being recorded. My answer to her was not a timid one. I did not back away from her frightening expression as I remarked to her that I was not an attorney, but that the plaque on her desk clearly read that she was a JUDGE, and that by definition she knew what she was legally capable of doing, it was not up to me to make the decisions which were already made for all of us having been set in case law many years before. (Did I mention that my mouth has gotten me into more trouble than most?) I told you being honest about myself may prove to be a difficult task. Faith in the justice system, faith in the statutes, faith in the fact that I knew she had to be controlled by someone, led me to answer her in the manner that I in fact answered her. The results of my answer, faithful as they may have been, were devastating. I lost my kids temporarily, I was held in contempt for my outburst, and it took two more years and three lawyers later, to force the hand of the judge to do what the laws said she must do. Faith is likened to food for me, it's something I have to have, but it doesn't always satisfy at the time that I want it to be satisfying. I have to wait just like everyone else.

If I were to be completely honest about it, I would have to admit to you that I never wanted to teach a single student, not ever. I wasn't going to be a teacher. Teachers were underpaid, never thanked, and hardly ever respected beyond the 16th week of the semester. I knew I hated a few of the teachers I had growing up. I couldn't wait to blow out of their classes, and away from their tyrannical rule! Teachers represented to me those who had grudges to bear, students to flunk, and people in subordinate positions to chew on just long enough to make themselves feel that much better in the first place for having chosen a career without a path. I was never going to be a teacher, I was going to be a lawyer. Thank you judge, thank you. Through her unlawful misuse of the laws of the state of Oklahoma, she was able to force me to give up a dream, only to dive into a whirl of light. I can't tell you now, how many times I have believed in someone more than they have believed in themselves—to work with them, show them the various ways and methods of success . . . and then, when the light bulb glows just above their heads . . . . miracles happen. I may not ever stand in a court room and defend an innocent mother of three, but I can say without regret that I have taught more than a couple of hundred of these women, and in the classroom I have far more say, far more ability to make an impact on the lives of their children and their children's children if I can guide them down the road of success through learning and applying the strict rules of grammar, literature, writing, and research. I am a teacher.

Chapter Six

Even writing this book is a test in faith. I really did not have a good time of it. When I think about it, it is as if someone didn't want me to start the book, let alone to finish it. My first thought of course, was to wake up in the mornings and sit at my home computer, write a few lines every day, get the book started, maybe get a few ideas from the novels and great books I have sitting perfectly still on my bookshelves. I would want to read a few of them first, and get a feel from the various successful authors how to write, what to do with styles, you know, steal a few ideas. I sat up the desktop, put a new screw in the chair because I had remembered that it would flop around on me when I sat up straight; all the things you do just to prepare yourself to work a little. When I turned my computer on it would literally take about 11 minutes for it to boot up and I couldn't force it to run faster when I yelled at it. I don't know about you, but I use hand gestures, dancing moves, facial expressions and even deep-throated threats when I want my personal home computer to obey my verbal and keyboard commands. It absolutely refused. Sat there as if it had the right to mock me. I showed it, I called my guru student, the one I caught skating through English the entire semester; however, he was able to rebuild every computer in our lab class, downloading free ware, taking off unnecessary materials and files. He was constantly tapping away at the keys and seemed lost inside his little world . . . I nearly cried when I had to stop him long enough to go home to his beautiful wife. "Hey, John, remember, class is only three hours once a week . . . . you actually have a life. Oh, and you have an essay due next week too, it's on Blackbeard." I won't tell you what John deserved on his essay. I gave him an A. He worked it over and over and rewrote it, finding ways to improve himself on his language skills. My home computer, following the semester, became a breathing monster when he was finished with it. I swear it could bake cookies if I asked it to. So why wasn't it working now? In a word . . . . Caity.

"John, she did it again. She found a way to hack into your password and she's downloaded Spyware, SWAT this and SWAT that, and every other means of tracking down government agency information on criminal types . . . like herself!"

"Don't worry Professor, I'll be right over." John was such a great student, he had paid someone to finish his essay on Blackbeard in record time; just so he could help me! What a guy! "John, when you come bring that movie you downloaded last week, the one my kids said was too gross for me. I'll make the decision."

"It is too gross for you Professor." he added

"Fine, get me another one, they can't have all the fun."

"How about 'Finding Nemo'?" he asked

"Sure."

While John decided my computer was fried and needed his undivided attention for a few days, I couldn't wait. I needed a computer now. Reuben had one. I could use it, or so I thought. It took a little faith on my part to go into my son's apartment to even use his computer. Most of the time boys are a little messy, and from time to time they even leave things about their apartments that they wouldn't want their moms to find. My son fits the bill when it comes to the mess; clothes on the bathroom floor, cards thrown on the table, pizza boxes everywhere. I used to think he used Little Caesars as a decor theme, until I realized that he was simply avoiding having to take the oversized boxes three city blocks to the nearest dumpster. Why can't apartment managers understand the need for more big blues? It only makes sense, put a few more dumpsters on the premises and there would likely be less cockroaches, less mice, less mess . . . maybe I can get a grant to study this theory. They give government grants out for everything else.

I'll have Caity hack into the Pentagon again and find out. She owes me.

Reuben plays a game with me. I told him I would be using his computer so he set up his apartment to be "mom-ready" as he called it. When I walked in the door there was big wooden sign pointing to his room, on the sign he had hung a paper message it read: "Don't look in the box on the left side of my closet." Another paper message was on the refrigerator, it read: "Don't ask whose beer is in here. You don't like her." I opened the door of the refrigerator, I knew my baby boy hated the taste of beer. Why would he allow someone I didn't like to bring over her beer, and if he did, why would he tell me I didn't like her. Why couldn't he let me think he was keeping the beer for a friend, or for that matter, maybe I wanted one. I looked inside, and all I found was another note: "Made you look! You know I wouldn't do that!" I didn't look in the box in his closet. I thought maybe he'd have stacks of books in the box. Proving to me that he was actually reading. If that ever happened I don't know what I would do. I like thinking to myself that I actually know my son. The day he reads for pleasure may be the day my heart gives out for the last time. I left the box alone and said a little prayer for my son, or rather for his future. "Dear God, give him hell. Make him the father of twins exactly like himself . . . no, make them eat more if that's physically possible, and God, when they visit Grandma, make them pick up their clothes and pizza boxes. Why should I have to go through this again?"

Reuben's computer was in his room, crammed between the wall and his king size bed. That's when it hit me; why did he have a king sized bed in a 12 x 11 room? Why did he have a king sized bed when I only had a full? Why did he have a king size bed? Who gave my son a king sized bed? Note to myself, ask Reuben about the bed and find out why he has a better computer too, he doesn't even know John. I sat at the desk, pushing the chair back as far as the edge of the bed, and realized that my stomach was literally touching the cabinet that held the computer. How in the world was this going to work? I'm not that big of a woman, but I was squashed between the bed and the cabinet, trying to get the computer to turn on, boot up, and obey my every command. My arms could wave, at least I had that. What did he have downloaded on this machine that took it forever to start up? I can go to CONTROL PANEL, I can look up what is to be added or removed, but I don't have a clue as to what the files are, or what importance they carry in terms of whether or not I'd fry the machine if I took them off. I decided to sit on the edge of the bed and simply lean over to type. Extending my arms, squinting to see the monitor, I realized that this simply wasn't going to work How in the world did this boy do anything on the computer? Every time I would try to type something on his keyboard little pieces of pepperoni or what was left of one popped out of it. Maybe he thought he was suppose to feed the electronic mouse or something. The screen went blank after a while, and it was obvious to me that he had placed a password on the machine just in case his friends wanted to do a little porn searching. The password screen wouldn't disappear. I tried everything I could think of: FOOTBALL, TACKLE, PLAYBOOK, PIRATES, his number, #63, nothing. I went the route of the only other interest in this boy's life: PIZZA, BURGER, FOOD, TACO, I knew he didn't know how to spell LASAGNA. Note to self: Get Reuben a twin sized bed. Second note to self: Laugh! Where would he put the other half of his king-sized body? I suppose as time surrenders itself to the rest of the world, and I am cognitive enough to notice the thirty-five cent increase in bread at Wal-Mart, I hadn't really paid that much attention to the fact that my baby boy was actually big enough to play linebacker for the state Championship football team . . . . oh wait, that's exactly what he was! Yes, third note to self: Thank God for little boys. Password? What was it? I tried the only thing I could think of at this point . . . PASSWORD, Bam! I was in, but to no avail. The boy didn't have Word or any other sort of writing software. At least I knew he had a relatively safe home to live in, he was eating, sleeping well, and wouldn't be able to write nasty notes to me online!

My quest to write continued and I found a friend with a nifty little lap top, but not until after I had driven about 300 miles inside the city limits tracking down a few of them that were reported in the newspaper, or from what I was told when I called every electronic store in the book. "Yes, we have laptops for under $200.00, they sell rather quickly, but you can see them if you . . . . oh, I'm sorry, we just sold out. You can try our competitor." I did that. I called every competitor in the area. My favorite was a guy in a little house on the south side. He was a bit spooky. I thought I liked him because he spoke with a little accent, he was always looking from one side to the other, and when he invited me into his tiny little entry way he asked me to remove my shoes. I didn't of course, pleading it as against my religion to put myself in the clutches of a would be murderer . . . he thought I was funny too. I walked past a graveyard for keyboards, an arsenal of mice, (do you call them mice if there are more than one?) It wasn't long before his pit bull "Blue" came out to see what I was doing. I realized Blue was all business and I stood perfectly still. "Did you go somewhere that I should be concerned about?" I called out to the little man. A voice rang out from under the house, perhaps a basement. "No, I'm in the cellar. I have a laptop somewhere down here. Don't pet the dog. He's really not very friendly." I believed him. Blue believed that I believed him. I prayed. I do that. I pray a lot. "Dear

God, you remember Blue. You made him when you made all those other demons that you cast out of your Heavens that sultry afternoon way back when. Could you please tell him the story of Daniel in the lion's den, and how you will get around to feeding him later. I'm not really . . . ."

"Nope, couldn't find it. Must have sold it." Nothing more. He didn't offer any names of his competitors, he didn't ask me to call again, he didn't say a word. I stood there for about a time span of 20 seconds wondering if it was my turn to speak, or if he was going to ask me something. Finally, I spoke. "Well, thank you for looking." He reached his hand out and took Blue by the collar, I backed away. I drove away, I finished my prayer . . . "Thank you God! P.S. Don't ever let me be that stupid again. Amen."

Niki and Eric have been married about 17 or 18 years. They have kids like mine, all too smart, too pretty, and too busy to be bothered with parenting. I step in from time to time to remind one or the other of them that they actually do have to listen to their mom or dad. When I do they think it's strange, but not one of them has ever been rude or disrespectful. I would hope that if my children were saying things or doing things inappropriate (God forbid . . . . hahahaha) that either Niki or Eric would step forward to pop one on the side of the head. That would be more of Eric's style, Niki, I'm afraid would try to reason. Why do people with her intelligence even think it's the correct method? I love Niki! Educated, beautiful, thin, (not skinny, she hates being called skinny) and a talented marathon runner. My feet hurt just looking at her. Eric, on the other hand looks like the Gorton Fisherman! Big-bellied, brawny, gruff, and bearded. I'm convinced these two met at a Halloween costume party. She thought he was . . . the Gorton Fisherman, and he thought she was an Angel. He was right. She married the king of the wharf, and they moved to Oklahoma to be close to me. I know they did. Somewhere in the back of their minds they hated living in Boston, hated the seven years they lived in Greece too, they were thinking out loud I'm sure "Somewhere out there is a land of beauty, grace, treasure untold, and there must be a talented and creative friend just waiting to be found." (Leave me alone, let me have my fantasy!)

They moved to Oklahoma because it was cheap and I lived here already. Besides, I am talented and creative, they do love me, and they loaned me their laptop! About two days into the writing process I noticed the computer had a software problem that I couldn't fix, and I had to give it back. If it wasn't one thing it was another. I couldn't get the time or the computer to write this book. Everytime I turned around I was being forced to give up a laptop, my own machine was incapacitated, my son's was impossible to figure out how to use, and I was losing the two weeks I had set aside to write. Two weeks. Can you imagine? Thinking about it I have to laugh. Authors of any success at all will write how the books they are working on take them years to write. I didn't have that luxury, I'm one of the poor American citizens. In fact, at the time of this writing I was not only an Educator in a poor state, making very little money, I had been fired from my position because my dog Faith had appeared in a nudey magazine. I'll write more about that in a subsequent chapter, but to tell you the situation I was in, I was unemployed, without enough money to feed my family really, looking for work, typing on broken or unusable machines, trying to afford a laptop I couldn't locate, and all the while saying to myself that this is a great book. It really is a great idea. If I can just get it out of my head and onto the screen. What screen? The problem was that I didn't have a computer. Where am I going to get this screen and will it work when I get it? Faith people. Faith. You gotta have it. If you don't look to a higher power to help you, you truly are on your own, and in my case it wasn't a good bet. I wouldn't bet on me. The last time I tried to do anything extraordinary I found myself standing in the unemployment line again. I have these really great ideas when I teach, its just that sometimes they don't work out. Like the time I thought I would get to work early so that I could get a few things done. Thinking back I remember now that my boss had told me to come a little after noon, I remember that now, but at the time

I walked in on him doing a bit of cocaine! Fired. Right there, I was asked to leave. I don't think I was even allowed to get my things. He threw a few at me, but to say that I was given the opportunity to gather them would have been overstatement. Yes, I called the police, I made a report. I was still unemployed and I was still standing in line thinking to myself "Don't go to work early, don't go to work early." Things happen to me that never happen to anyone else, and for the life of me I can't tell you why. I can tell you this . . . it has made it impossible *not* to have faith. Faith is the proof of the fact that I do actually believe that no matter what happens to me I'm going to be OK. I believe that now because I've been OK for so long. Somehow I always wind up living and usually intact. There is something to this belief thing. Faith is good. Faith is very very good to me. Like Toby Keith says "Get ya some!" I think he was talking about babies, but still, it works with faith as well.

Niki and Eric encouraged me to try again with the stores in the area, and I found one. This one. I've taken it back a few times to have the keyboard replaced, Word needed to be installed, it needed to be given a new battery and floppy drive, but other than that it's a fine little machine. I had faith, and at times that requires an enormous amount of work as well, but nevertheless, I am writing, and the book is being written. Finally. I hope you like it.

Chapter Seven

I wanted to talk about some of the things that my family and I went through before we were given our dog Faith. I want you to understand that we're a normal, typical family, that things happen to us, and that because we have faith, things work out. It isn't always easy, in fact, it never is easy. Where is that guy who told us that the world was fair? Where is he? I want to pop him in the mouth for lying. We were kids when we learned to play fairly. We were told that we should be fair, that it was the right way to be. Where this is true, I also tell my kids that it won't usually be given back to you. You play fairly, and you are to be as fair as you can be with others, but to expect less from them. I'm not a pessimist. If anything I am an opportunist . . . I believe we can take the experiences given to us and find a better way. My favorite boss in the whole wide world, even better than when James Garner was my boss, is Mr. Moler. Mr. Moler, an attorney for the City of Nichols Hills, told me not to look for justice in the courthouse. He said it wasn't there, he said we make it. If we wanted justice we had to be willing to be the one that creates it for others in our lives. He couldn't have been more correct. Without fail every trip to the courthouse proved so opposing, so out of the ballpark when it came to fairness, that I often wondered why we have a judicial system in place at all if the judges are not going to be forced to use case law as precedent. If indeed they can arbitrarily decide for themselves what they will hear and what they will not hear in terms of the guts of a situation.

Having faith is a difficult and essential part of being a parent facing an uncaring, biased, unwilling judges of this world, real or in position, who have been assigned the duty to listen to people lie as they explain their reasons for having drug the one person they swore to love into the courtroom, now accusing them of immoral perpetude or worse. The job itself has to be damning, it's no wonder we don't have more of a suicide rate among our bench warmers, then again, perhaps they get their revenge by creating as much havoc from their vantage point onto the lower classes who dare to interrupt their lives with trivial matters such as accusations of child abuse, endangerment, lack of child support, broken promises, and worse, kidnapping. Mustering up the faith it takes to face the days in court is in and of itself a feat. One that takes more than what I personally am able to do on my own. Faith in my friends was important at this point. Faith isn't just about trusting and hoping in God, you've got to put your faith in others as well. You have to believe that they were sent here, put here, to help and that they have the abilities to help when you can't. I remember once I had a friend in court, a man I had never met. I was crying, the judge was displeased that I showed my emotions in her court, I was taking up her time. He came over to me, held my hand, looked at the judge and asked her to be patient, to wait just a minute, that a mother's heart was breaking before her, and that it needed some time. I never saw this man again, I probably never will again, but he was exactly what I needed when I faced the opposition.

In my personal case, my ex husband had been ordered to restrain his current wife from physically beating and hurting my daughters. He had been ordered not to use corporal punishment on the girls, and I had been ordered, (yes, ordered) by the court, not to call the police again when I suspected that my daughters had been beaten, abused, or neglected. How a judge in any state, for any reason, can think that he or she has the right to tell me I can't call the police is beyond me, but it is of record, that is exactly what she ordered. I was told that I was not to call the police again because I had called too often. With every call I had placed to the Oklahoma City Police Department I had been given a number, an assignment number, proving that the officers who had responded to the call had actually completed their task. Problems arose when one police officer merely said he had made the stop by the house on Rambling Road to see if the children were safe. I had called after a neighbor had called me to say that their father's wife was pulling Caity into the house by her ponytail, and that she had been kicking her in the legs while she was pulling her inside. I called the police and according to the report he filed, he had spoken with my daughter and nothing of the sort had taken place. I had not seen the event, but upon later conversations with my daughter the event was true, all except the part about the police officer questioning her. This became a concern of mine and I reported it to the correct authorities. The next thing I knew, I was being ordered not to call them if there was another problem. The logical conclusion is that the officer realized his mistakes but was unwilling to fess up to them. Instead, I was the bad guy. I was calling unnecessarily, I was overreacting as far as they were concerned. To tell the truth, I had called the police a great many times to see if my children were well and being taken care of because my children were calling me telling me that they were being left alone without food, that they were being hit by their father in the face, or on the legs with the buckle end of a belt for not doing the dishes. They reported that his wife had kicked one of my girls in the stomach for yelling at her son when he poured grape juice on the dog. Not having custody was not an option for me. I sought it at every cost, order or no order, I called the police when my daughter Laura called me screaming into the phone that this woman was again kicking Caity in the head out in the backyard. No neighbors came to her assistance when she screamed at them over the fence, however, one of the neighbors called the police anonymously, saying their father's wife was always doing these sort of things. Dale, for his part, quickly loaded the kids into his van after the police spoke with him, and drove away so as not to have to deal with the situation. The police responded to my next call because of his behavior, but I have to believe they did so under the influence of my neighbor's call, not mine.

It may be best to explain how things could have gotten so far out of hand. Dale and his new wife Bella lived in a house on Rambling Road. The house we had purchased after we had remarried. This was the house we were suppose to have started our lives over in. That didn't happen. In the original divorce decree he wanted the house, and it was understood that we would have *joint* custody of the children. Because I was returning to school, a mere freshmen, knowing it would take a few years to become established on my own, I allowed him to have *physical* custody, but not *controlling* custody. We were to make every decision about our daughters together. It was never a question as to whether he would be free to marry, or date, he had promised me, the girls, and even my parents that he was not going to disrupt the girls' lives with dating or marriage because they had been through too much. That lie lasted about as long as it takes a butterfly to breathe and die. Within sixty days of our divorce in 1997, Dale had met, dated, shacked up with, and married his new wife, a married woman who was pregnant with a third person's kid. Dale, a man who had at least claimed to be against abortions not only paid for her to have an abortion, he used money he had withheld from me to do it. He had owed me a couple of thousand dollars for the down payment on the house, or rather he had owed it to my parents. With this woman now living in the house, given her past of being married at least two other times, and of having been kicked out of at least two places for non payment, having been fired for alleged embezzlement, and knowing that she was under a doctor's care for extreme depression, and even a bipolar personality, I wondered what Dale must be thinking. It had been myself who had called Dale to let him know that she was married to a man in another county. Dale didn't want to use his own money to investigate the woman he was about to marry, and he knew I would do so without a problem because he intended on keeping her in his house. This was literally less than two months after we had divorced.

"She's married to a Tommy Beldner. It is registered in Stephen's County."

"Did she divorce him? She said she divorced him." he wanted to know.

"Her petition is filed, but it hasn't been finalized." I added

"Why not?" What's the hold up?", he asked

"She's being accused of infidelity, if you can believe that Dale, seems Tommy thinks Bella is sleeping around on him, what do you think?"

"Shut up! I just asked you to see if she was married. I don't need your preaching."

"Did you know she was married to a J.D. Skymaker before Tommy? Did you know her high school principal said she was married to someone else when she was a junior? Did you know she was fired from a financial company because she allegedly embezzled from them? Did you know she took drugs for being bipolar?"

"Shut up! I don't give a damn", he continued, "She does what you won't do, and you left me, remember?"

"I left you", I declared, "because you did things I wouldn't do! You had an affair, no, you had a lot of affairs! I was just nice enough to forgive the ones I knew about before we got married again."

"Fuck you!", he exclaimed

"Not now, not ever again. Thank you. You're married to a married woman!"

Having a little faith was not enough. At some point I had to take more action than was allowed by the law, and finally, after a beating, a kidnapping, finding another attorney, being ran over by a van, and finding Dale and Bella in contempt of at least 20 rulings, I had my day in court. MY day! This of course didn't happen all in one day, but that would have been nice. I wouldn't have had to live through the months of hell had it been limited to a 24 hour period of time.

Chapter Eight

March 4, 2001, Bella's birthday. Dale "allowed" me to have the children, as if he thought he had a choice, it was my weekend. I wasn't "allowed" to pick them up until he said so, and when he made the arrangements for me to pick them up they weren't ready, and I was forced to wait outside in my car for over an hour. I took the girls home, we had dinner, we talked and watched a movie, and the next day I took them to church. Dale wanted them back before 3:00 p.m. as the judge had ordered that I could only have them for a limited time following an error of my legal counsel from a previous fiasco. Even though it was proved in court that the error was made, I was having to obey rules which were not only damaging to the girls, they were out of line legally. My time with the girls had been shortened and it had not been reassigned when the opportunity arose. This to me was a blatant attempt on the part of the judge to prove she was indeed in control as she knew there were laws she had to obey, but she could certainly control my life as it pertained to the girls, that is until someone stopped her. It would be up to me, up to faith to find that person.

When I had kissed the girls and loaded them up to take them home Caity crawled into the car with a grimace on her face. "What is it" I asked. She raised up her pant leg and showed me a big bruise just under her left knee cap. "What the heck is that!" I asked. "Bella kicked me because I wouldn't get out of her chair." I was furious! I knew I couldn't call the police, but I also couldn't continue down the road that would lead to me dropping my children off with that monster. I handed Caity the cell phone. "Call 9-1-1", I directed her. "Ask for the Will Rogers Station, and tell them we're on our way to the make a report of child abuse. Do it now." Caity made the call. Of record, she even stated to the 9-1-1 operator her name, where we were driving at the time, and that her mom wasn't allowed to call the police because the judge told her not to. When we arrived at the police station we were met by a man whose concern about me having been ordered by the judge not to contact the police was evident. "You mean to tell me that a judge told you never to call us again?"

"That's correct. I was told that I had called you too often. Now look!" I told him as I pointed to Caity's knee.

"I'll take care of this one personally." He promised.

He and another officer took Caity behind the thick glassed entry and into an interview room where he photographed the bruise and took her story. He told me that under no circumstances was I to take the child home, that I was to go to the emergency room of the Children's Hospital, and that she was to be seen by a physician immediately. I did what he commanded. I allowed Caity to call her father to let him know that she and Laura were not coming home that evening. As I suspected, he called my cell a number of times. Seeing his phone number appear on the calling ID I did not respond nor did the girls respond. It was the first time that Laura had actively chosen not to talk to her father. She wasn't used to disobedient behavior, even if it was for the best.

We arrived at the emergency room doors of the hospital and met with a triage nurse. She asked us if we could possibly come back early in the morning, as she was sure the wait would be several hours. They were backed up, and a bruise was important, but not important enough to move ahead in the line. I was immediately reminded of the times I had taken my children to the E.R. when they were understaffed and I was screaming for help. I understood her situation completely, and decided to come back in the morning.

Before I went back to the emergency room of Children's Hospital on March 5, 2001, I called my legal counsel. The same mad man that had made the critical error in court just months before which had led to this new beating being possible. He happened to be downtown and he made an effort to come to my office to speak with me. For a man weighing over 300 pounds he managed to dress himself quite professionally. When I had first met him he seemed caring, interested in my case, and willing to help. In subsequent months and even years since the custody issues were being heard, he became too involved with his personal work on issues not dealing with Legal Aid. He had made comments about being underpaid. I wondered if he wanted me to make payments to him personally. I never made any, but I wondered if I were able to if he would be more likely to help.

He rode the elevator to the 28th floor and looked out of breath. He acted as if being my lawyer was an inconvenience, that Caity being injured did not fit with his daily schedule. He was acting rather strangely. In fact, he was acting as if he wasn't wanting to be my counsel at all. Where he was appointed by Legal Aid, I felt that he had obligations to me, obligations he obviously was not interested in upholding. He asked the girls to wait inside an inner office. He wanted to speak with me. He read me the riot act on having contacted the police about Caity's leg. I reminded him that child abuse was still illegal in the state of Oklahoma. He was not interested in helping me, but knew he had some obligation to inform me that he would be asking to be releaved of his duties because I failed to comply with court orders. I knew something was up. When the elevator bell rang I ran down the hall and held the door open. He asked me to step aside. I asked my children to get aboard. He demanded that I wait for another elevator, I demanded that we all ride together. The man was furious. Caity looked him in the eyes and lifted up her pant leg exposing the injured knee. "See it!" she demanded. "See what she did to me." This was all the law required. He now knew first hand what had taken place, and he couldn't resign, not until the matter had been resolved. "Damn you!" he whispered at me. "Not today!" I whispered back.

When the emergency doctors took Caity into their examining room they found more bruises than the ones we saw with the naked eye. She was literally covered in micro bruising from her head to her legs, bruises of various sizes, shapes, age and distinction. The doctors asked about a specific set of bruises to her arm, how did she come to have them. Caity explained that a few days prior to being picked up from her dad's house, she had been screaming names at Bella, and that her dad had twisted her right arm behind her. He had then shoved her into a corner with force. This bit of information warranted a closer look of her face, where more bruises were found under the skin, visible by alternative lighting. These marks were consistent with having been hit in the face, or having one's face hit the corners of two walls joining each other. There were bruises on her left cheek and her little nose. Considering the house for a second I asked Caity if she had been shoved into the corner of the foyer by the laundry room. She said she had. This was enough for the doctors and a report was made. Unfortunately, I was unable to get a writ of emergency from my underpaid and overworked legal counsel. He instructed me to return the girls to Dale or he would have reason to pull out of the case. What choice did I really have? At least I had the DHS involved, and I had proof of violent behavior. I knew I had to get another attorney, a real attorney, and that thought consumed me. I made less than $22,000 a year, how was I going to afford someone that would actually be able to do more for my girls? Through faith. This one would be up to God.

I returned the girls to Dale on March 5, 2001, after work. I remember giving them both names and numbers of their guardian ad litem, Glenda Tucker, and made them recite the number back to me. I was certain that Dale would not allow them to call me again, and I didn't know how long it would be before he decided to obey the order of the court and not hurt the girls. What I was certain of is that he would be very angry when he was made aware of the fact that the girls were the ones wanting the investigations. They had given interviews freely to the DHS workers, the hospital nurses, doctors, people who were sitting next to us at the emergency room, and virtually anyone who would listen to them tell their stories. When I think about it I am compelled to recall Pat Benetar's song *Hell is for Children,* a song about child abuse and how parents train and teach their children to tell little lies to cover up the mess they have created. "Tell Grandma you fell off the swing." My girls weren't shy at all, perhaps Laura continued to apologize for her father's behavior, saying that he didn't mean to hurt them, or that he didn't know Bella was hurting them, as she explained how they were being hit, kicked, pinched, spat at, and being called names that no one should endure. Names a father should certainly never use and names he should never allow his wife to use with regard to his own little dolls. These things did not matter to him or to his wife. What they did next was criminal and inexcusable. Faith was hard to come by on March 6, 2001.

By faith Moses put forth his staff and God parted the waters. By faith John the Baptist shoved locust into his mouth and God made them tasty. By faith Robert E. Lee signed a declaration which in a nutshell, ended the war between the states but it cost him more than he could possibly have imagined. What was gained of course, was a treaty of peace, the ending of bloodshed across a nation whose morals, ethics, and beliefs were strongly supported on both sides of the Mason-Dixon line. By faith I called out to God asking him to find my children and to keep them safe when it was reported to me by one of Laura's little friends that she had not been to school all week long.

Spring Break 2001 wasn't for another couple of weeks. For Laura not to be present at school meant that she was sick. Her father refused to answer my calls, he had caller ID as well, and try as I might, I was unable to get the interest of my attorney. When my daughters hadn't called me from the house of one of their friends, which had become a habit I appreciated, I decided to contact the schools. Laura was attending a middle school where my son was attending. He was an eighth grader, she a sixth. The principal knew me, and was well aware of the current situation in Laura's life, as the strangest stories and scenarios were being told not only by myself to her teachers, the principal, the nurse, and to her counselor, but they were being repeated by her friends as well. Several of Laura's concerned friends went into the principal's office, or the counselor's office to report that Laura's father had thrown away her homework, or that he had snatched her out of their house when she was given permission by him just an hour beforehand to play. They were concerned not only for her safety, but also because she was telling them that she wanted to live with her mother. She was afraid her father might physically hurt Caity. Laura rarely mentioned that her father might try and hurt her. She was always and forever concerned for her baby sister. Ironically, it was Caity that fought back with each attack, heaving loose bricks at her perpetrators, scratching and clawing her way out of a ponytail hold; and even flushing diamond rings down the toilet when her more aggressive behavior was not appreciated.

On the morning of March 13th I walked into the office of Cooper Middle School to speak with Dr. Ronald Green, a man I have always admired, not only for his ability to remain calm in just about every situation, but because he was wise enough to listen to the children in these cases, rather than making decisions based on the tales he heard from either side of the parenting camps. Naturally, as the principal at their school, it would be difficult to make a judgment call based solely on one side of the story. Every story has two sides, and in this case, the stories I told had multiple and unusual endings. We absolutely never knew what to expect out of Dale Stickley. He was literally capable of such grand scale destruction that to even guess at his irrational behavior was an exercise in futility. He would say the same thing about me in court, he would produce documents which were falsified, not certified, and the police would trust him because he was so calm. I was afraid the principals of my children would believe him as well. After months of observation by a court ordered therapist and a very expensive psychiatrist, it was deemed in court that I was sound, that I had more traditional parenting skills, and a more stable lifestyle than that of their father. To be fair to Dale, it also showed that he had decent parenting skills, but that he lacked judgment concerning who he left the children with. The reports showed me to be argumentative, defensive, combative, and ambitious . . . OK, so what? I am, these were my kids!

The problem with the report was that the judge was unwilling to reverse her order for custody because it would mean that she had acted inappropriately. Even through the psychiatrist had also found Dale to be a liar, a pathological liar, and that he tried to manipulate the test several times, she wanted to wait until something extraordinary happened, or until the kids reached the magically age of 14 and the courts had no other option but to listen to them. This was 2001, and Laura was only 11 and Caity was only 10. Dr. Green met me with a concerned look upon his face. He was a father, a married-to-the-same-woman-forever type of father, and he was personally unable to feel empathy for me in this particular area. He knew that Laura had been missing from school, but he was bound by the state laws of Oklahoma to lean toward the custodial parent in these situations, which at this time was Dale. However, he also knew that as Reuben's mother I was completely aware of where my child was at all times, that he was encouraged to do his homework, that he was supported dogmatically at every school activity, and that I was very concerned with his progress. Dr. Green also knew from Reuben's reports that the girls had been taken and that they had not been allowed to contact me or anyone else because of the abuse Caity had sustained. Reuben had told his counselor about the hospital, about the reports of abuse, he assured the woman that the DHS was involved, and that the police reports were real. After the counselor spoke with Dr. Green, his answer to my question about Laura's whereabouts was simply that he did not have any idea where she could be, but that as soon as he found out he would contact the DHS and ask them to contact me. I also knew that he would find a way to let Reuben know where his sisters were as well.

Caity attended Northhaven Elementary, a school all of my children had attended before the final divorce. The principal at Northhaven was a belittling man, a man with an ego the size of Kilimanjaro, and in my opinion, one of the worst principals to walk into the Putnam City district. He and I did not get along as he was surrendered to believing ever insane but calm word out of Dale's mouth. It was true that he was a better actor than I am. I was unable to hide my emotions, I was unable to put on the face of pity, which Dale often did, claiming I was a victim of incest, that my history with drugs and alcohol was such that the children were taken out of my custody. Tsk, tsk, he would tell the principal, it is a grave shame that she was asked to leave the children and to never speak with them, she has had severe mental breakdowns and she simply isn't stable to be trusted with them. All this without a single report of proof. Where I was seen in the eyes of the highest ranking officer at the school as being a complete danger to my child, the only saving grace I had was the fact that Caity's counselor knew me from an acquaintance. She was Mr. Moler's friend, and she had taken the time to ask specific questions about me and my personality. Convincing the principal that Dale was not only lying about my person, but that he was indeed the culprit behind the missing homework, the bruises, and now the disappearing of my child, was another matter. Mr. Pansy, the principal, literally asked me to my face where my child was when I went to Northhaven to ask him the same question. I felt perhaps a friend of Caity's had been contacted. I had a police officer waiting in a car outside to help me if I needed it. He was an off duty cop that I had asked to be there in case I needed support. Mr. Pansy leaned over the counter and told me that he was ashamed to say he knew me. He didn't have a clue as to the depths of my character and I needed a court order to be on the premises in the first place. When I asked him to produce anything, anything at all with that sort of restriction, he came back with "The children's real parent has told me what you have done to these children." I think Mr. Pansy needed the cop outside the door, because I was just about to kill him with my bear hands.

I had other dealings with the teachers and administrators of Northhaven Elementary following one of Dale's little visits. It seems he was successful in hiring Laura's fifth grade teacher Mrs. Laya Wilcox to do a little tutoring for Laura during the summer. Interestingly enough, I had custody of the girls during the time he had promised Wilcox the tutoring gig, and considering she had previously lied on stand in court about Laura's whereabouts the year before, having believed Dale without evidence, I chose not to allow her to tutor Laura. By this time I had graduated with an education in Liberal Arts. I knew more about teaching my daughters than this young, limited experienced teacher with her general education, and I told her when she called seeking the employment check that I would be canceling the order. I had not given permission to Dale to make these arrangements, and as far as I could tell, Laura had not learned anything remarkable during her fifth grade. She was now in the summer of her sixth grade, going into seventh grade, and without the least bit of knowledge of standard grammar, literature, social studies, math, or history, things that Laya Wilcox was commissioned to teach her. Of course, Mrs. Wilcox's rebuttal was that Laura would not pay attention in class, that she had many tearful breakdowns, and that she was simply unable to be a participant in class. She had recommended that Laura be held back. Nearly every one of the girls' teachers from the time they were in the 2nd and 3rd grades respectively, had wanted to hold the girls back because they refused to participate. I knew my girls. I knew what they were and were not capable of performing. The performing part was the problem. Do you blame them? Who could ask a kid that was being thrown around at one house, protected by the law and a forbearing mother at the other, to become a willing participant in school. I'm amazed they have survived at all, and when I look back on the days they were kidnapped, or shall we say "taken without permission", by their father in 2001, I am sure it was their own faith that brought them through the days and nights of being abandoned by their father to stay with friends who were given strict instructions, withheld from their mother. Can you imagine?

Chapter Nine

No parent should fear that walking into their child's school will be a situation where a police officer will be called to escort them out immediately. No parent should be shunned by teachers and administration on the word of a man who had no evidence to support his outlandish remarks and comments. Nevertheless, I was not given free speech at Northhaven elementary until after the girls were returned from what has been called by them the kidnapping. On March 26th, 2001, I received a call from Caity, she was at school. She had walked into the office and demanded to use the phone. When the principal wouldn't let her use the phone to call me she immediately began to scream out loud that she had been kidnapped by her father, that she had been held in a house without a phone or internet to contact me. That she had been left with people she did not trust, and that she was going to call her attorney Glenda Tucker. Caity has never been one for subtlety. I don't know what Dale was thinking when he brought them back. He had intentionally kept them from me over Spring Break, which was my custodial time, he had kept them from me over two weekends which were my custodial periods, he had not been with the girls even for a day. He had left them in the care of his friend Byron Barker, a man he had personal knowledge of being a wife-beater. The wife Byron was married to in 2001 was not the woman he had physically assaulted in 1997, but Dale had been his friend, coworker and even his boss in Tulsa since before 1995. He was the man who stood beside me when I remarried Dale, he knew of my love for my children, and yet Byron believed Dale. Whatever Dale told him, however he managed to convince Byron not to allow the girls to contact me, was successful. What was Dale thinking when he dropped Caity off at Northhaven 19 days after having kept her captive? Did he for one minute believe she would be quiet, or did he believe she would not try to call me? He obviously miscalculated his youngest.

I had already anticipated that he would be brining the children back this particular day. I felt in my heart that he understood that I was not playing games with him any longer. On March 23rd, when I had not heard from my daughters I walked into the courthouse and onto the 4th floor with a writ in my hand that I had typed and was about to file. It was an explanation of my perspective of the kidnapping. I had taken Victoria Reddling, my personal spiritual counselor, and a church friend with me on the previous weekend and had contacted the Oklahoma County Sheriff's department to be an escort for me as I attempted to rescue my daughters. Victoria was well aware of all of the things I had been going through since my divorce. I had joined the singles group of the Metropolitan Baptist Church, a church just up the road from where I lived. Victoria and her roommate Katherine Martin had been strongholds for me since the very beginning of my custody woes. Both women had prayed for me and had come to the courthouse on several occasions to be with me during my appearances. In fact, the day I lost custody due to the error of the court, was December 5, Victoria's birthday. She is certain that this would be the worst birthday she had ever have. I hope she's right. I hope she never has another bad birthday as long as she lives. Both women have been pillars of strength for me and for my family. I think of my entire church family when I remember the old saying that it takes a village to raise a child. Katherine, small, petite, stern, and intellectual, can be juxtaposed in her countenance by the fact that she loves to speed around town in her sexy little convertible, her long brunette mane flying in the wind. Were it not for Katherine's keen mind and quick wit, I would never have found the faith to continue my fight. She refused to allow me to stop. She knew the hearts of my girls and where they needed to be.

It was believed on March 23, that the girls were in Stephen's County with Bella's parents even though this claim was denied by Bella, her parents and her ex-husband, who I had become acquainted with since I had given a written testimony for his case against her for the custody of their son. Of record, an Oklahoma County Sheriff, Officer Abernathy, contacted Dale using his cell phone. He demanded that Dale bring the girls back to the house on Rambling Road, he demanded that Dale surrender himself to the County on charges of kidnapping. Dale told the officer that he could "fuck himself" and that the "girls would never see their mother again". This was enough for Sgt. Abernathy to file a report which was later used against Dale, and was instrumental in reversing the order in Judge Cauldron's courtroom a little under four months later.

Faith. This is the stuff it is made of. I had to sit there in the driveway of the house I was suppose to be living in raising my children, and I had to put up with a man who not only abused our relationship, but I had to sit there and listen to the officer tell me that he could only file a report. Of course, I knew I could not force the Sheriff's deputy to conjure my girls from thin air, but I had to remain calm, not only because it was the civil thing to do, but also I knew that faith was worked by God, and believed by me. Faith is something we have to have when we absolutely can't change the situation. We can't force life to happen the way it is suppose to happen, but we can have faith that God is in control, that He can change things, that no matter what is happening He will be the one to fix it and to make it tolerable again. There's a really cool verse in 2 Chronicles 20:12b and it says "We don't know what we are doing, but our eyes are on you Lord."

What was Dale thinking when he dropped Caity off at the school? God had made a little me when He created my last spawn! She was never going to allow him to get away with kidnapping her. She was never going to allow him to take her away from the internet. This child lived to hack her way into the world of the unknown. She was fully capable of grappling with Bella by this age, and this is the one reason she was hoisted away. Dale was going to be going out of the state and he could not take the chance of Bella or her new baby Morgan getting hurt by my darling devil-of-a-kid Caity. She literally stood in the foyer of the school screaming until someone took her aside and let her call me. To think, all Mr. Pansy had to do was to do what Dr. Green always did . . . . listen to the kid!

Friday, March 23rd, before the scene in the foyer of the Northhaven Elementary school, I was making my own scene on the fourth floor of the courthouse. The place was packed with suits. I was wearing a pair of Rider jeans and a pull over I'm sure, as I usually never dressed up on Fridays at Mr. Moler's office. Actually, I never dressed up at all when I worked for Mr. Moler, except on the days after he and I had engaged in a little disagreement. At times like that I wanted him to think that I perhaps had a lunch time interview. There I stood at the clerk's desk with writ in hand, and it occurred to me that the best way to get a great lawyer was to ask for one when 100 or more of the species was standing around me. Did you wonder where Caity got it? I asked loudly "Does anyone know a damn good lawyer. I need one now! My ex husband has kidnapped my children, and is extreme contempt of court, can anyone suggest a name?" A man from the left side, about to file a motion for continuance in his own case said out loud and very pointedly "Anita Sanders!" About that time a mumble was heard throughout the room. This room is a long and deep room. Mumble turned to rumble, and I wrote the name Anita Sanders down. "Would you like for me to call her for you?" came another voice from behind me. "She's kicked my butt a few times in the courtroom." Then another voice chimed in, and another, it seemed this Anita Sanders was something of a legend. I was ecstatic, until I realized that if I couldn't afford her I would be wasting her time. "I don't have any money." I said to the last man who had offered to place the call. "I don't know that she takes money." He said. This was the most surprising news I had ever heard in my life. He continued to say that part of the thrill for Anita was the fact that she really enjoyed beating the daylights out of attorneys who represent people they should not be representing. He said that Anita was well known for her bartering and that if I had something of value to offer her that she might very well listen to me, and at the least, she could do it for the kids. I let him place the call.

Anita F. Sanders didn't look like a monster, when my friend Joseph Hamilton and I visited her on the morning of Saturday, March 24, 2001. In fact, Anita stood about my height, she was considerably smaller by weight than I, and her *fangs* weren't showing, her claws must have been retracted, and when I took a quick look around her office I didn't see any ball collections, at least not the kind that were proclaimed as being her favorite. To me Anita seemed quite pleasant. She offered John and I something to drink, even a bit of pasta salad she was so proud of herself for having been able to concoct alone without help. She mentioned that her maid had taken leave and I wondered if I could use this bit of information for bartering purposes; at least the thought occurred to me. I was willing to beg. Anita's game plan was simple, she wanted me to write down everything that had happened from the day Dale and I broke up for the last time until the very day I walked into her office. Simple yes, but impossible. I explained to her that the highlights alone would fill a volume or two of the worst rot you could ever imagine reading—albeit true! She wanted most of the highlights, with a special emphasis on what was going on this very minute with the kidnapping. I held in my hand the report from Officer Abernathy, which Anita found not only amazingly stupid on the part of my ex-husband, but incredibly detailed. She stated that she had never heard of an officer taking the time to actually fill out the report so well, this man must have found Dale particularly upsetting as well. I suppose it was a good thing that my ex could be so terrible to more people than just myself, in the end it was his undoing.

Our court plans were simple as well, Anita was prepared to file an Emergency Order on March 26, 2001, asking for an immediate reversal of the last Order, and giving me permanent and full custody of the girls based on the facts surrounding the kidnapping. How could it be jeopardized, what could possibly happen to stop the action . . . a van, that's what. The morning of March 26, 2001, found Caity being dropped off at the school just about the same time Anita and I were walking to the courthouse. Dale was expected to show of course, given the gravity of the situation, his attorney was contacted, however, since there wasn't a 24 hour notice given his attorney expressed Dale's decision not to be present. However, a separate Order and court date was scheduled for the same case in the same court room on the same date. He didn't have a choice in showing up or not. He was expected to be in the courtroom. As Anita and I walked across the street to go to the courthouse we were physically struck head on by a moving van. The van it turns out was rolling at about 20 miles an hour. It was the same color, make, model, and year van as that of my ex-husband. Naturally I screamed when it hit me somewhere around the knees. Thoughts racing in my mind of being killed by the idiot rather than him facing the inevitable, people do worse you know. I was dumbfounded! Neither Anita nor I were knocked to the ground, but we were pushed against each other, beaten a little and bruised by the van. I remember my brief case hitting me in the upper arm somehow, and from the mark it left you would have thought I was punched by George Foreman. Immediately Anita informed the driver to stop. He wanted to drive on. He was driving without a license, his left arm was broken and in a purple cast, while his right hand was busy holding a cell phone! The man was rounding a corner and had no intention of stopping. Though he wasn't my ex-husband, the shock of the van being so close to the same type of van Dale drove, it took quite a while for me to get over the vivid imagines that my mind was trying to conjure.

When the EMTs arrived Anita and I begged off going to the doctor because we weren't hurt too badly, however, in time my arms really began hurting, as well as my back and upper thighs. Our case was postponed of course, and the only thing that was ordered without my presence was against Dale, he was ordered to never leave the girls with anyone besides me. Though he was not present to hear this, a copy of the order was sent to his attorney. Not that he obeyed the order, he was always one to believe and behave as if he believed that he was above the law in these matters. To him the judge was useless unless she was ruling in his favor. Wouldn't that be grand? I wouldn't have had to run to the bathroom every 10 minutes I was inside the courthouse if I felt that the judge would be ruling for me on every issue. As it was, I couldn't be too far from the stalls. It was incredibly annoying to me that I would be able to take kidney stones, three natural births, and so many other events in my life, but standing in the stale musty courthouse while waiting on a ruling that should be in my favor, but was often not, made me sick to my stomach . . . often.

Journal Entry:

May 1, 2001

"This day made me sick. I don't know how much more of this I can take. Judge Cauldron knows that Dale left the state. She ordered him to leave the girls with me if he did that again. Why can't this just end. He's such a liar. Here we had an emergency order because he left the state again and let Bella watch the girls. Caity called me to say she was getting hit again. I called Anita. We had the order in place before the judge and then she doesn't show up! We got a new judge, he wanted to give Dale a chance to get back from Virginia to testify. Hello, he wasn't suppose to leave again without giving me the girls. This is so simple. He can't leave the state without giving the girls to me. He did it again. Put his butt in jail for contempt . . . again!!!"

Giving up my faith was never an option. Falling flat on my face praying for answers was the best option I had. I couldn't possibly think of asking for help from any one else but God. To even think there is no God would be impossible. If there was no God there was no hope. If there was no hope there was no reason to do what it was that I was doing, which was trying to get my little girls back home. Prayer was not enough, faith had to be present. Without the faith, the active work which comes with faith, and the active works of others who carried the same burden of faith for me as I did for myself, the girls would not have had a chance to be free. The girls needed me, they begged for me to take them away; no one listened to them or to their cries of course, they weren't allowed to listen. I wasn't alone in this sorted mess. Everytime I went to court I heard the same stories in the corridors. Everywhere you turned someone was screwing someone they used to love and cherish over. Someone wasn't paying child support, someone else wasn't following orders. Why?

Why can't people do what they're told to do, and why can't the law be enough to make someone do what they're suppose to do? Under the laws of the state of Oklahoma, the girls were given a guardian ad litem, someone to represent them in court. This doesn't mean that Glenda actually listened to the girls either, in fact, Glenda was their second GAL. She was better than the first one they were given, that woman, Carrie, had been asked to leave the case when my first counsel was fired. If I could have fired the GAL I would have, but it was made perfectly clear to me that the only way to make sure I was given a different GAL would have been to drop the case in its entirety. This was before Legal Aid was involved, and had I realized that the lawyer I was dealing with was as inexperienced at this type of law as I was, I may have been wise enough to file a protest. Surely there had to be another way to have a GAL assigned to the case. It was 1997 when I first realized I would need to seek custody of the girls, and the first GAL was appointed. She was white, thin, middle aged, a smoker, a liar, and I suppose worst of all, she was uncaring and if the case wasn't going the way she anticipated she would intentionally leave a file in her office forcing the judge to reschedule the court date. This was her way of making sure she made it to her nail appointment! That may sound bitter on my part, like something I would simply say because things

weren't working out for me, however, I was extremely
new at this game, so I followed her. I followed her
all the way to the salon downtown and I watched
her. I heard her making the comment to the
beautician that she would have been there earlier
but she had a case to "deal with". She stated that
she had left the case file in her office, and how the
judge had rescheduled the hearing. I wanted to
expose her, instead I asked my attorney how I could
have her reassigned. Her answer was to release her
as my attorney, and to reopen the case, asking my
judge for a second GAL. She was at least kind
enough to mention that the judge would probably
say no, but that I was to insist on grounds of the first
GAL's contempt for the law. Like that would work,
but I thought I would try anyway.

When you're as green as I was about the matters
of divorce and subsequent divorce issues as I was in
1997, you really don't consider the thoughts racing
in and through the judge's mind. She wasn't happy
to hear that I had fired my attorney. She wasn't happy
to see that I had reopened the case the next day, and
she certainly wasn't pleased with my explanation; that
I had been directed by my attorney to do so because
the GAL was incompetent. "Are you stupid Ms.
Stringfellow?" asked the judge. "Are you so completely
stupid that you would believe your attorney would
have anything to do with reassigning the guardian ad
litem? She has nothing to do with assigning and

reassigning these people. You are either incredibly stupid, or incredibly gullible, and either way I'm inclined to believe that you are incapable of raising children properly." This to me sounded as if the good judge had already chosen to give my daughters to my ex-husband based on the fact that he was able to pay for a better, more experienced attorney, and because he never once argued with her. Why should he have argued with her, she was ruling in his favor, and believing the lies he was able to get by with. Her ruling to have us all examined by a psychiatrist should have been enough for me to realize that her idea of getting rid of the Stringfellow case was to see to it that I spend more money than I could possibly come up with. She darn near succeeded too, and she would have except for one thing—faith. My church was behind me. There were prayers and prayer meetings. There were literally meetings where the people in my singles department did nothing else but gather at my friend Joseph Hamilton's house to lay hands on me and to pray over the situation. These people knew me. They knew I was not always the most quiet and calm of the two parties involved in the case, but they certainly knew I was the one telling the raw truth. Perhaps the fact that it was so raw was the problem. Judges and lawyers alike don't relish having to listen to details as sensational as to say that this man had actually beaten his children on the sides of their legs, their backs, and on their faces with the buckle end of a belt in their own beds while they slept. They didn't want to hear how he had left a 6 and 7 year old more than a mile away from home and told them to walk home because they had seen their mother at the store and wanted to be with her. If no one was willing to listen to the children, there would be no hope. Glenda Tucker was the best Cauldron could do for the girls. She is a middle aged, shorter than I am, African American woman with a soft and steady voice She was not a smoker, and she seemed more or less dedicated to children and their causes. She may not have been friendly to me at first, it was her job to be impartial when it came to the parents, and I know I annoyed her more often than not by insisting that she listen to the girls. She met with the girls, and after the initial meeting Glenda accused me of manipulating them because I asked the girls to make lists of things they wanted to talk to Glenda about. In her world children talked freely about issues or nothing was wrong in the first place. This not being the case with Laura, I asked both the girls to come up with lists to provide Glenda a more precise picture of what was going on.

"Ms. Stringfellow, are you telling the girls what to write, they are telling me that you told them what to say."

"No, I asked them to make lists, and I helped them create their lists, in that I helped them to write 1, 2, 3, and to list out what it was they wanted to talk about."

"Did you correct their spelling?"

"Yes, I did correct their spelling. Is that a problem?"

"Yes, it is a problem, it looks as if you are telling them what to write."

"Well, I'm sorry, I didn't want them making spelling mistakes."

"Next time Ms. Stringfellow, let the girls decide what they want to tell me."

She acted as if I were sitting the girls down and instructing them on what to tell her. I told them to tell her about the spankings, yes, but I left it to them to describe when and how they were spanked. If these guardian ad litems truly believe that every child will speak freely about details, they haven't been around children enough to know that the first thing a child will do in these cases, no matter how badly they have been hurt, is to protect the parent who is doing the damage. My girls were unwilling to tell stories that could put their father in jail, but at the same time, they also realized that the stories would not be heard if they were not told. They realized that they could not live with me if they did not tell Glenda the truth. I think at first it was Caity that told the more gory of details. She was somewhat closer to the situation than Laura. Laura, for whatever reason was still under the impression and hope that her father and I might reconcile. It was her duty to try her best to see to it that Bella was blamed, leaving the doors wide open for her father and I to be together again. My poor baby, she should never have had to be placed in that situation. Glenda told me over and over again that Laura simply couldn't tell on her father. To me this was evidence that there was more to tell, to Glenda it was a brick wall she simply couldn't get past. She was inclined not to do anything to help the girls if Laura was unwilling to help herself. It was time for more drastic measures and DHS was called in to do what Glenda either couldn't or wouldn't do.

Chapter Ten

Like Glenda, our DHS worker Ellen was not in the Jude-camp immediately. Looking back on her decision to be impartial makes much more sense now, but at the time I couldn't even imagine how anyone could want to give Dale a chance to explain himself, knowing what I knew about him. Then again, it was usually only my word against his word, as the girls were either not being listened to, or when they were being listened to they wouldn't tell the secrets deeply embedded in their hearts, as they didn't want to see their father getting in trouble. Faith is a funny thing, it actually requires a person to do something, and doing nothing doesn't always mean a person doesn't have that faith, it simply means that person isn't willing to help themselves. Sometimes you just have to let go and get it done. This is exactly what Laura was doing, she was doing nothing to help herself, therefore, it was hurting the cause; nevertheless, God wasn't finished with the case or the cause. Through Laura's non communication about the matter He was able to show Ellen the depths of the damage being done. The only problem, as it always is a problem, is that the process took a great deal more time. This time allowed Dale and Bella the opportunity to do even more damage.

One of the first things Laura was willing to discuss with Ellen, Glenda, and even Dr. Champlin our court ordered therapist, is that her pets continued to be given away. This is such a major issue that I simply can't let it go without saying that with each new pet she would receive she would end up having it taken away, given away, thrown away, or dumped on the side of the road for absolutely no reason other than her father was tired of its animal behavior. If the dog or cat pooped on the carpet, Heaven forbid, it was given away or the gate was left open intentionally to allow its escape. This action was nearly always done while the girls were in class at school. They would come home only to find their beloved dog or cat missing. A search was made of course, Dale tried to look and act concerned, but when the time came for Laura to discuss these events in her life with the proper authorities her guard for her father was finally severed. He could beat her, yell at her, take her toys, sell her clothes and dolls in a garage sale without allowing her to retrieve them with her own money. He could cuss at her friends, he could take her food away from her, or force her to eat things he knew very well that she hated; but take her animals away and

Laura refused to protect him any longer. With great detail she showed Ellen a final list. This list was not created in any way by me. This particular list was a creation of Laura and Laura alone. It contained the names of over forty animals that Dale and Bella had given to her and Caity over the course of a couple of years, only to have them given away, thrown out the door of the car in front of the girls, taken to a dump site, or let out. The list was simply names, names without faces, fur, or stories if the list was merely read. As Laura held the list in her hands she became angry, upset, and eventually she became straight-faced, looking into the eyes of the DHS worker hoping for justice, wanting to put an end to something that was causing her so much pain. "Doc, Diamond, Lady, Wishbone, Jasmine, Jade, Sadie, Max . . ." and the list rolled on. "This one we had about three days until Dad decided it was ugly. This one bit Morgan on the hand when he pulled it by the tail. This one didn't do anything at all, but Caity got a D on her spelling test and dog begins with D. I guess if she had gotten a C the cat would be gone." I couldn't do a thing to help my daughters. Every week with my visitation, if I was granted the privilege, I was told about another animal, another story. I began telling the girls to not become attached, not to go through it again and again. They couldn't help themselves, they were little girls and the animals were always small, furry, cute, and so playful. Dalmatians, German

Shepherds, a Collie, a Beagle, a Jack Russell Terrier. Next they'd come home to find one missing and another to replace it, it developed into a stressful, wishy-washy wondering game of what to expect in the house or the backyard with each new day. "Trouble, Coco, Patch, Gus, Lucky . . ." and the list goes on, "Dakota, Bear, Caesar, Simon . . ." Ellen had heard enough. This time it was going to be over. This time I had the weight of the law, as well as the height, breadth, depth, and long arms of it on my side. She couldn't do much more than make a recommendation, but due to the extreme mental and emotional stress Dale was imposing on the girls by taking away their animals, and replacing them so often, something could be done. A pattern of neglect and abuse was established. Lists can be a good thing too Glenda, lists can save the world.

Faith, or the act of faith, isn't always associated with bad events. We can't think of faith as being the saving tool that comes to our rescue when we're depressed, sad, or hurt. If faith was apparent only during troubling times we would only be expected to use and have faith when we were going through some sort of trial or tribulation. With faith I find there is a constant need to renew communication with God. Why talk to Him only when you need something desperately. I wouldn't want my own children to ring me up on the phone only to beg me for something, or to blame me for what was going on in their lives. I find that faith, or having faith is something so ingrained in our souls that we do it, have it, use it, whatever you want to call it, on a continued basis. Take for instance the time that Caity was doing cartwheels on the four inch beams surrounding my parents' house. It wasn't that I believed she would fall, I had faith that she was going to be OK. I didn't believe she would fall, I remember thinking that I would fall if I had tried to do something like that, but I remembered being six and climbing over a very large fence with a large yellow sign hanging tightly to its webbed encasement. The sign read (but I couldn't read at the time) RESTRICTED AREA, DO NOT TRESPASS, FEDERAL PROPERTY. Wow, big words. I knew I could climb over the fence, I had a mission to accomplish. There were bones under the ground and I wanted to find a few more to show my friend Willie D. He didn't believe me when I told him that the bones were in there, just sticking out of the ground and everything. How could he not believe me? Wasn't I his best friend? Wasn't I with him when we found the great big crawdads in the creek and I was the one that ate the head off of one to prove I wouldn't die? That was me, he had to believe me when I told him I had found a real live dead bone of an Indian! Faith. I would get over the fence, I would get to the wooden house about a city block into the field, and I would dig up another bone to show Willie D. He was the one too scared to go this way, he had to go around the creek, over the cliff and around the park. Man, that took forever, and you had to ask permission of the lady who lived in the blue house to use her backyard to get to the field. Sometimes she said no if her husband was home. I wasn't about to take that chance. Up and over. Fast like, no one looking, and thank God for that handy-dandy sign I could put my foot on to hoist myself over anyway! Faith in one's self can be very liberating! You don't always have to have faith only in God or in things not of this Earth . . . heck, I had faith in the people I wrote to asking for help to publish this book. I needed the money, I asked, and I believed it would happen . . . you're reading the book aren't you?

My first grade teacher was another strong faithful influence. I don't want to get her in trouble or anything, but she wasn't exactly orthodox. She didn't exactly go by the rules, not unless the rules included carrying your shot gun to school and keeping the bullets in your pocket. She let me hold the gun once but it was too heavy and I dropped it on my foot. It wasn't loaded, she had already used the final shell on a rabbit we had come across on our way to the school. Mrs. Adelaide Earp lived just across the street from me. She was at least sixty-five years old when she started walking me to school in 1967. Earp was one of those pioneer women you see and read about in books so old the pages have all turned yellow. She was short but I was too. She was stout, about as strong as the oak trees in her back yard that she used to climb into the get the acorns to make whistles out of. She had those hose that hung around the base of her thick trunk-like legs which where shoved into the black clog boots that had hooks instead of ties. My hair was long I thought, but I had no idea how long hair could get until the day I saw my first grade teacher pull the hairnet off her round, tall bun. Down to the ground her hair fell in dark and gray strands in the most amazing demonstration of hair-letting that I had ever seen. Country music fans remember Crystal Gale's hair and the way it hung behind her when she posed for pictures, or stood on stage, literally having to flip it behind her to even see where she was walking. Adelaide Earp used six strong hair pins made of tortoise bones and shell to hold her mass up on top of her head. I can't imagine the weight she would release each evening, but I saw it often when I snuck up to her bedroom window at night and watched her comb through the long train. It was yet another thing I couldn't convince my best friend of. He didn't have Mrs. Earp as a teacher, and living three doors down from her made him nervous in the first place. She never did take to walking over to his place to drag him to school by the hand. I was the only kid in the entire school who had that privilege. Why me? I couldn't tell you except I know she had been my three siblings' teacher and maybe they had told her stories about me. That was the only thing I could think of. It certainly couldn't be the way I crawled under the street through the sewer traps, or how I rode my bike at neck-break speed past the red eight-sided signs reading STOP . . . whatever that meant! Five and I couldn't read yet. By six she saw to it that I did. What stopped me from crashing into the side of an on-coming car or bus? Probably my mother's faith because I didn't have any at the time. I just have dumb luck to hold onto.

The book of Hebrews goes on and on about the faithful in the stories of the Bible, how they did this or that with faith and to be honest I wondered when I was little how the author of the book even knew about some of the stories that he was writing about. There weren't books, television, movies or even newspapers relating these stories. Maybe he was in Mrs. Earp's first grade class because she talked about Abraham, Isaac, Jacob, Joseph and Moses all the time. Abraham, at least in my opinion, had the most faith. Joseph sat in a well waiting to be rescued, but when he was he was taken care of. Jacob had to raise twelve sons but in order to get them he had married the wrong woman once (how do you do that after being in love with someone seven years? I'm thinking Leah and Rachel's dad was the best confidence man ever!) Jacob raised twelve sons, and he had two wives and two concubines to help, nevertheless, raising twelve boys couldn't be easy . . . however, he wasn't asked of God to literally sacrifice his one and only baby boy. Abraham was.

I've thought about it, I couldn't be an Abraham. I did notice, and I often notice, that when God requires the blood of a child he never asks the mother to do it. He asked Abraham, not Sarah. Can you imagine what Sara would have said to Him if He had asked her to take the life of her only son? I can tell you now that she had absolutely no idea where Abraham was taking her baby boy that sunny afternoon when they found themselves at the top of the mountain preparing to obey God's will to the fullest. God is the Father of Jesus, Mary is His mother. God did not ask Mary to give up her first born. God knows all too well the hearts of the women He has created. I can think of one or two women who could give up their children and to this day I abhor them, creating in my mind the deepest pit in Hell for any of them who could say or do anything to harm their own children; so why does God expect us to be able to follow a command that could actually cost us the lives of our children? Some questions simply have no answers? St. Augustine asked a great many boundary questions in his confessional journals and I suppose I do as well, however, I know that the best answer I can give you is that God has never required this sort of faith from me, and probably because He knows my answer. I would rather die myself. Whether this is wrong or right, I can't tell, but without the mentioning of my faith's limitations I would wonder about such limitations. Where does my faith end? Where does any faith end? For that matter when does it begin? I remember being two years old and being in the hospital under big plastic curtains. At the time I had no idea that I was dying of double pneumonia, but I do know that I didn't worry about that part of it. The beans were fun to pop in my nose. The doctors and nurses came quickly into the room every time I did it. They held me, kissed me and kept me happy when my parents couldn't. Beans aren't exactly an ordinary tool of faith, but I knew how to make them work. Faith? The angels must have been signing the petitions against me, asking God to find another soul to protect! Something tells me there really is something to penance and angels probably have to pay it as well. Any angel falling short of his or her angelic duties has to watch the two year old babies of the Earth! It's a rule! That could very well be why the angels smile so often in the pictures I see of them. "Thank you God for not putting me in the nursery! Sing Hallelujah!!"

Faith at 6 weeks standing in the snow.

Caity: Poet, Author, kid.

Faith and Ean playing at 3 months.

Anchor Linda Cavanugh broke the story on June 23, 2003, on
KFOR-TV Oklahoma City, OK.

Reuben: Faith's original rescuer.

Maurice Ernest Gibb, the man I wanted to marry at the age of 6.

Laura: Actress, singer, sister.

Rocker and Poet.

Looking forward to the future.

Chapter Eleven

In time faith prevailed. In time even the great Dale Stickley had outstayed his welcome in the courtroom of Cauldron. With the various contempts adding up through kidnappings, missed visitation, horrible actions and reactions to orders, an Emergency Order was filed in the case. With Anita, Ellen, Glenda, and the report of Dr. Lora Champlin, our therapist, in the file, I was given full and permanent custody of the girls on Caity's 11th birthday, July 25, 2001. Ironically, Cauldron had yet another lapse of good judgment when she ordered that Dale had a couple of days to gather the materials and goods for the girls to be delivered to my attorney's office on July 27. Rather than demanding that the girls be turned over immediately, she allowed him 48 hours to say good bye, and to prepare them for this permanent readjustment. Caity was at home with friends that morning, and with Bella. She had woken up to a bright stark sunny sky, and the faith that she would be holding me soon. When Bella asked her what she wanted for her birthday, Caity answered "God is giving me my Mom today, just like He gave me to her eleven years ago." The comment caused Bella to hit Caity on the shoulder with a cooking spatula. It didn't matter any more, Caity and Bella both knew that they would forever be free of each other in just a few days. That didn't stop Dale or Bella from creating as much havoc or damage as they possibly could for the remainder of two days. Every shirt, skirt, pair of pants, undergarment, toy, pillow, or belonging owned by the girls was stuffed into black plastic bags.

If the girls believed they were being taken to my attorney's office they were wrong. Dale delivered less than ten percent of what belonged to the girls to Anita's office. Instead he took their things to the nearest Good Will store, leaving them outside because the doors were locked. Had I known what he was doing I could have driven by and retrieved the gifts my sisters, mother, friends and family had given to my little girls. When Laura and Caity realized that they were without clothes, toys, china dolls, and jewelry given to them they cried, but it could not dislodge the joy in their hearts as they danced up and down the courthouse halls, literally shouting "Mom got us back! No more Bella! No more!" It was actually a little unraveling to tell the truth, it felt both good and bad to hear them feel so relieved to be away from the man who had been in their lives since the beginning, but there are times when I would have died to give them this freedom. Faith prevailed. There's a woman we call Grandma, (her real name being Martha Washington) she works in a little Italian restaurant called Ricolettos downtown. No one really knows how old Grandma is. She's ageless, she's dynamic, and if nothing else could be said about this African beauty wearing sparkling berets, one thing can certainly be said: She is a woman of faith. I found myself going to Ricolettos for more than the inexpensive pizza on days I simply couldn't take the stress of missing my children. Grandma would come out from behind the counter and she would hold me. She would raise her hands into the air and proclaim through uninhibited faith that the Lord would deliver to me my babies. She called them the "Blessed Babies". "Lord, bring the blessed babies to this woman! Lord, I cry to you, YOU, YOU GOD, are the only one able to deliver us, you are the one God, you are the lone and the only, through our faith, through our prayers you hear us. Lord today bring your peace! Lord, be with these children, these blessed babies. You know where they are today! Bring these babies to their mother!", and as I cried and I prayed along with her, I secretly wished I was black. I wanted the freedom that wasn't taught to me in my white Baptist upbringing. I wanted to throw up my hands and wail. I wanted to let God know that I believed He could do this! Thank God for faith, loud faith and quiet faith. It's all good. I love you Grandma Washington.

July 27, 2001 found my daughters in my arms again. Reuben was even happy to see his sisters which wasn't always the case. Even Reuben knew what it meant to have the girls back, certainly it meant he would have to share me and my affection, but he knew the torturing would end. Reuben had been eleven when Dale had spanked him for crying when the Green Bay Packers lost the Super Bowl to the Denver Broncos. John Elway received a gold and diamond ring, Reuben was placed in a hope chest at the house on Rambling Road when he wouldn't stop crying. Dale sat on the box, a wooden chest that my own father had made my son, until the crying stopped. My son, my baby boy was unconscious in a wooden box, and I think I was at a restaurant having cheese fries with my best friend because it wasn't my weekend to have the children. This event led to the three year battle for permanent custody of the girls. As soon as the event was reported to the police Reuben was removed immediately. For the life of me I can't understand why all three of the kids weren't removed from the house on Rambling Road after that day. Reuben knew all too well what it meant to have his sisters home again.

END OF PART ONE

PART TWO

FAITH, a Little Dog

Chapter Twelve

I woke up this morning with my legs and feet trapped under the blanket and under the weight of a yellow dog draped ever-so-lazily over the back of my calves. Since Faith has been in our family I have learned to lay flat on my belly when I go to sleep and I stay that way, unmoving, no rolling over, no turning whatsoever. We have a code in our family. We simply can't disturb the dog (any dog) once he or she has settled and given up that lingering sigh which tells us that the dog is ready to relax. I don't know how the code began, but it has been an endless source of laughter for us. I can literally call out to one of the kids and have them utterly interrupted to ask them for a cup of coffee, to turn down the stereo in my room, or to give me the book at the base of my bed because I can't possibly disturb the dog. Sometimes they give me face about it. I can be annoying when I take the code to the extreme. Why it doesn't work with the cat is usually because the cat won't stay in my lap long if I bellow out to the kids for assistance. Dogs don't care. Dogs in my family know better than to look the least bit rattled. Laying in one spot after scratching the blankets to make them just right is the beginning of the signally of the code. "Dog in the lap!" I call it out just to let them know. This gives Laura the initial clue that I am about to call her to get my coffee, a book, or to anything else I might need. Disturbing the dog is never an option! Mornings can be an exception to the rule, the dog has rested.

Each morning, just like this one, I get up in a stupor and ask the dogs to get off of me. When I say that I ask the dogs, I'm really more or less demanding them to get off of me. Faith lays on top of the covers and between my legs, pinning me to the bed, while Matrix lays beside me under the covers, his long, fat, black dachshund/beagle body stretching from my head to my knees, and my face is usually at the wrong end of the dog. Often times I don't even require an alarm time, a fart from Matrix is signal enough for me to get out of the bed and take the dogs to the backyard. Why do we indulge our animals? Why do we put such an emphasis on the loving of these mangy, half breed creatures who have been spoiled beyond any degree of sanity? Because in my house the list of animals is much shorter, and to give one away would be virtually an impossibility. Matrix has his own miracle story, one that begins during the time that the girls were in Dale's house on Rambling Road. I had decided to lease a little house just around the corner from the girls so that it would be easier to keep track of them. Their friends began walking to my house to be with the girls on my weekends. Some weekends when it wasn't my weekend to have my own daughters I had three or four other *daughters* who couldn't resist the smell of chocolate chip cookies. I usually ended up with Helen Stakker and Ashley Tubble for at least one or two nights a week with or without Laura and Caity to play with them.

Matrix, Faith's adoptive brother, was found at *Pets and People*, a wonderful no-kill shelter in Yukon, Oklahoma with dedicated volunteers and workers who have it in their heads to find good and permanent homes for dogs and cats who are either abandoned, strays, or about to be killed at the city shelters. Pets and People have a very rigid record keeping system, and they keep pictures of each of the hundreds and thousands of animals that make their way through their doors. Matrix was officially called *Lambert*, and he was considered too sick to be sold with any guarantee. When he came to the shelter he had worms, ringworms, and other puppy problems. He wasn't over six weeks at the time, and therefore he wasn't for sale. Why is it that whenever I write that down, he wasn't for sale, that in the very next sentence I'm telling you how I talked the shelter's keepers into giving him to our family. We pleaded, we begged, we even promised not to worry about the guarantee. We wanted a dachshund. "He's only part dachshund." They countered. "He's enough dachshund" I offered. "He's sick", "I have experience with sick dogs. I can medicate him. I'll let you medicate him, I'll take him to whatever vet you want me to take him to." In secret I knew I was going to be leaving Pets and People with a dog that day and I really wanted another weenie dog. They have always been my favorite. "Fine, take him to Dr. Diane Delbridge. She's here in Yukon, and we'll know if you don't go to her. I'll personally come to your house and get Lambert back if you don't do everything she says to do."

I made the promised agreements and I took my little sick tri-colored, mostly black, mixed breed dachshund with me. There was no way I was going to call him Lambert. I thought about the latest most up to date names, and not one of them struck me as being cool or good enough for my little dog. He was awesome. He was going to make it, he was going against the odds, but then again, he was in my family, that was a normal and every day thing. He would have to get used to it, and he would have to be above reality. That's when it hit me. I'd call him Neo for the character Keanu Reeves played in the Matrix. He wore mostly black, he was sleek, fast, a great fighter. He had to believe he could win, he had to believe he could make it through the toughest of tough times. That was it, I was going to call him Neo. My children decided Matrix was better, and therefore he was renamed, but from time to time when no one else is paying the least bit of attention, I whisper in Neo's ear and I tell him how great of a dog he truly is.

Matrix wasn't exactly accepted by our two cats Sting and Tigger. Cats are cats, you can't argue with them, they always win because they decide before the argument begins that you're wrong and they simply walk away. I threatened to withhold food once to make my point, however, I realized that my leg could actually be considered a choice of nutrition to a cat whose food had been withheld. Matrix wasn't like that. He would be mine, he would listen to me, he would obey my every command, and he would love me no matter what happened. Cats are cats and they don't have to follow rules. Why do I have cats? I can't remember the reasons behind the first one I brought home, nor can I figure out the reason I keep one. Wait. I've never had just one. I've always had more than one of everything when it came to animals, cats were no exception. Tigger, the gray tuxedo older brother of Sting (Tuxedo Black) made the first sweep around the kitchen to examine the new invader. His decision would satisfy Sting who actually never left his perch from inside the cabinets to investigate. Leave that to Tigger, thought Sting. If he doesn't like the dog we'll kill it, it will be over in day or so. Matrix must have said or done something right because he lived. He did however, make the terribly stupid mistake of trying to eat out of the cat bowl, which brought about the hardened swipe of a clawless foot across his face.

I could see the eyes of my loathsome gray cat as he looked at me in utter disgust! "I could have used my claws at this moment, thank you!" Still, with or without claws the point was made, and the docile pup took his rightful place in line which was right behind the backside of the younger brother Sting, a fatter, darker version of the king, Tigger.

I can imagine the conversation between the three went something like this:

Tigger: Eat out of our bowl and you will die.

Sting: Tigger, don't you think he has to eat? Perhaps after we eat would be appropriate.

Tigger: The woman may not leave enough.

Sting: She seems intelligent enough, she knows she must feed him as well.

Tigger: HE isn't even a cat!

Matrix: May I interrupt? What exactly is a cat?

Tigger: Kill him. Kill him now.

Sting: Let him be. We can train him. He can be . . . he can be our pet!

Tigger: Pet? Are you suggesting that we pay attention to it?

Sting: Him, he's a him. I looked. He can be our slave actually. Would that make you happy brother?

Matrix: What exactly would I be doing as this . . . . slave, is it?

Tigger: Did we speak to you?

Matrix: Well . . . no, but . . .

Tigger: Shut up!
Matrix: Of course.
Sting: See! He's learning already. Good dog. Very
       good dog.
Matrix: Are cats really dogs?
Tigger: Kill him . . . . kill him now.
Sting: You amuse me Matrix, you amuse me. Come
      and sit.

From day one the dog was trained. I never had to tell him twice not to eat all of the food in the bowl they shared. Why it never occurred to me to get two bowls for the different species I don't know. I had a big bag of cat food and he could eat that for a while until pay day anyway. He learned quickly to wait until he was given the right to eat, and he learned even more quickly to hide behind the considerably larger butt of String if he wanted to avoid another face swiping from Tigger as well. Sting found it quite interesting to tease his older brother by walking between he and Matrix. Dr. Delbridge was another story!

"You know you can't feed the puppy cat food. I found cat food in his stool." They always know don't they? You can't get anything past them. "You need to start the dog out with Iams and keep him on it. I'm going to insist." I nodded my head. I agreed to do this until the keepers of the shelter were completely satisfied that my more than thirty-five years of pet owning were enough to satisfy them. They were quite diligent in their follow up routine with this little mutt.

Weekly visits were required as well as progress reports. Matrix was given injections, pills, lotions and creams to rid him of the ringworms. If Pets and People had any idea that I had owned devil-cats they would never have allowed me to take the dog in the first place. Cats can be the source of ringworm and with his extreme condition, it would have caused quite a problem. They never asked, I never volunteered. I suppose I could have answered an ad in the local paper for a dachshund, but I didn't have the $300 plus to shell out on a dog at the time. Besides I wanted a mutt. I don't really trust purebreds they can turn on you! (laughs)

The house on 88th, just around the corner from the girls, was owned by a small, blond, foreign woman from Poland. She, among other difficulties, could not speak English well enough to understand that the house was in need of repair. My rent, as a matter of fact, was suppose to be going toward the lease/purchase of the house; however, repairs such as were needed were never introduced into the bargain. When I refused to pay rent until the drains were fixed, the water heater replaced, the chimney repaired, and the foundation cracks sealed, the owner of the house did the unthinkable; she sold the house out from under me. It was amazing! I came home from church and a process server was at my door. He handed me a summons which stated I was required to appear in court. I fully understood her reasons for taking me to court for the repayment of rent, and it would give me the opportunity to speak with a judge who not only understood the laws, but could understand the English language which the contract had been written in. As is par for the course, they sided with the owner of the house because in his opinion, her lack of the grasp of the English language exonerated her from anything binding. I couldn't believe it, I was being asked to leave a house I had poured money into, had intended on purchasing and had a contract stating that these facts were real and immediate. This new disturbance was critical to the lives of my pets of course, as the only credit I had was bad credit thanks to having no money after paying three attorneys to get my girls, and there was absolutely no way of gaining any additional credit to purchase another house in the area. I was forced to move to an apartment and with that move, I was forced to find homes for my pets as well.

It wasn't that day, or the next day, but soon after the court hearing we were packing and moving to a small two bedroom apartment with hardly enough room for our furniture, let alone the hopes of what it would mean if and when I won custody of the girls. Between the divorce issues, school work, working full time, and trying to find homes for my animals, I believe the word "stress" was used on a routine basis. Not to worry I told myself, I always land on my feet. I always seem to be OK no matter what happens to me and this was just one more thing. But it wasn't just one more thing; it was the giving away of more pets. There were no dishes needing to be done, no homework missed, not a single reason to say good bye to something we loved except a nasty woman who won the flip of the coin in a court room which in my opinion should have seen that she knew enough about the language to draw the contract up in the first place; it should have upheld for me. In time the woman lost her war. The people who leased the house after me took her to court and used my contract as proof that she did in deed know more about the laws and rules of the language in order to submit a subsequent contract to them. They won the ruling, and in turn, because the owner was so negligent, they now reside in the house that should have been mine. Nice I could help.

The basic plan was easy enough, though the weather wasn't cooperating, we decided to place an ad in the paper for all of the animals and to interview the prospective callers. When we finally found the couple who were more than willing to meet us half way, over 15 miles, to adopt our now 8 month old puppy, we were happy to see that the woman was pregnant. It meant that they truly wanted our doggy for the family and that he would be loved and cared for. I explained to her husband that Matrix was a rather spoiled dog, and that it wasn't his fault altogether. We were the culprits, having allowed him to live in the house, and we slept with him. I slept with him for the most part, but from time to time he would leave the bed sometime in the early dawn hours and crawl under the covers of the girls if they were staying with me over the weekend. They completely understood. That's why I was taken completely by surprise a few months later when I received a call from a man claiming to have found Matrix in the parking lot of Tinker Air Force Base, a military base about 20 miles from my house, but in the opposite direction of where we had taken Matrix to live. Spring months had melted the snow and ice which had become such an obstacle in finding him a new home in the first place, perhaps now that the weather was better, and the baby born, the family had decided they couldn't take care of him any longer. We'll never know why this seemingly loving couple lost Matrix to the base parking lot. The man turned out to be a Captain in the Air Force, he said that he would be willing to keep Matrix, that he in fact had been a dachshund owner as a kid, and that Matrix was more than welcome to share the little house he kept on the base. Great! My little dog was now going to be a fly-boy, and I could rest again that he was being cared for; although it did bother me to think that in the several months that had passed between the January deliverance to the lovely couple, they had not seen fit to get him a new tag—I had explained that his rabies shot was due in April. The only way the Captain could have reached us was to contact the vet, and she must have given him our number as we had continued using Dr. Delbridge after we had prayed Matrix to health and had what we felt was a successful adoption of him. Thank God again, the good Captain was going to be more careful with out bundle of love. Or maybe not.

Another few months passed and the custody battles raged. This was the time of the kidnapping, the beatings, the belting, the bruising, and the bullying of Bella. Matrix was far from my concerns as I had found homes for the brother cats the day I had found his first home. The cats, being brothers, and being tuxedo in costume, were no problem at all to find homes for. Both brothers were cared for immediately, kept fat and happy in the arms and hearts of a family living right outside of Oklahoma City with a 13 year old son who had cancer and needed more than one kitty to love. As I cried I handed the box of furry feet and tails to Penny Makington, prayerfully asking her to be careful driving through the blizzard conditions; Tigger was prone to car sickness. We surrendered a couple of nice bath towels for the cause, just in case. After a few initial calls to tell us the boys were doing fine, we lost contact. From time to time I think about Tigger, more so than I think of Sting. Sting had become Reuben's cat, more or less, and Tigger was the one to bother me more often with his insistence that I had made the worst mistake of my life for bringing the mongrel into his life. I wondered what the good Captain was doing with my most precious boy now. That was some time in the Spring of 2001.

July 27, 2001. Custody was finally mine, and the girls couldn't be happier. We hadn't had a chance to celebrate Caity's 11th birthday and in doing so I allowed them to pick whatever place they most wanted to go. I didn't care if it had been Disneyland! I would have found a way to do it. Lucky for me they wanted to go to the unusual choice of Yukon's Pets and People. An odd choice, since they knew we lived in a tower apartment and would never be allowed to keep even fish! Rules were rules in this place, and they were forever checking to be sure no one was breaking them. Pets and People it was! We could scoop poop to their hearts' desire, we could walk dogs, help hold the dogs being bathed, and we could kiss on everything with four feet and fur. Sometimes strange thing happen, and so it was that when we walked through the doors at Pets and People we were followed by fate.

We walked into the front door of Pets and People on the brightest of days in late July. I asked to see the manager and explained to her that my darling little girls, who I had just won complete, full and permanent custody of, wanted to celebrate by cleaning out cat boxes, walking dogs, and giving baths. She understood. To say that this sort of thing happens all of the time would be an overstatement, but there are times when kids can't help themselves. They have to pet a dog or two. This was one of those times. We were ecstatically happy, and the dogs deserved a bit of that joy. Let's walk 'em all. About thirty or forty minutes into the session one of those strange God-did-it moments happened. Matrix, our Matrix, came around the corner, pulling his collar off, letting loose of the keeper whose job it had been to gather him from the bathing room and to deliver him to his kennel cage. "MATRIX!" I heard my daughter Laura shout. "LAURA!" you could almost hear Matrix cry. If I had not been the believer that I had been I would personally never have believed this story if someone else had told me. What are the odds of the dog we had to give up over six months before would be standing in the very foyer of the one place we had found him in the first place? Hadn't he been adopted, dropped off, adopted again? Now he was back in our arms? The keepers explained that he had been brought to them just a few months before by the good Captain. Seems after he had told us he would be taking care of Matrix he received orders to go to Germany. He couldn't take the dog. We had changed our phone number, but had not given it to the vet, as we had not taken her any animals, we didn't have any animals to take. The Captain decided that Pets and People, though a good long drive from Tinker, would be the best place to drop off Matrix. He was surprised that he would not have to pay any drop off fee because Matrix had once been Lambert. The records from Dr. Delbridge's office had confirmed that Matrix was a Pets and People pup, and as is their ruling, they always take back one of their own. But that had been three or more months? Had poor Matrix lived in kennel cages and on hard tile floors since the early Spring? No. It seems that according to the records, Matrix, as he was officially being called now, had been unsuccessfully adopted three more times. With each adoption he was returned before the end of the week! "This dog barks if you don't let him in. We have neighbors and we can't have this." Then there was "This dog is a mess! He won't sleep in the yard, he won't sleep on the laundry in the laundry room, he actually expects to sleep in MY bed, and he wants under MY covers! I don't think so!" The last one was the kicker. This particular person had been counseled on all of Matrix's strange and spoiled ways. She adopted him, paying the standard $55.00 fee, and was told that for whatever reason, if she needed to bring him back, and that she more than likely would be, she would be refunded all of her money. By this time Pets and People had heard it all.

Susan Mario, the last "owner" of my darling doggy was the victim of the fart-in-the-face routine one too many times. She understood that he had his own particular schedule. She understood that he wanted to go out in the mornings, pretend he wanted to go out in the afternoon, fully expecting you to stand in the door waiting on him as he walked around the yard, scoping out the smells and dealings of the yard, but that he had no intention whatsoever to do any real business. She even understood that he only ate dry cat food, and that he was never going to sleep outside, in the garage, in the laundry room, or under the bed. It was going to be in her bed, next to her, and under her covers. That did not bother Ms. Mario in the least. She had been a dachshund slave before. What she could not bear were the morning fart fests. They start at about 7 a.m., and if one is wise they will simply turn their head, tuck the covers under the dog, or put him out, as it really is an indication that he needs to be relieved. Mario's answer was to harshly scold Matrix, and to threaten to return his tri-colored butt to the shelter. Ordinarily this would have been effective I suppose, to an animal who couldn't go on living without their owner, but Matrix, obviously, had other places to fart. He was in the hands of the only one that could know, and to know without doubt, that the two little girls in his life from the beginning were going to be given back to their mommy, and that this very day they would be returning to the one place they had met just a little while back. Faith doesn't always have to take the defensive—offensive works as well. We took our little dog home and home is where he has been ever since. On my lap, under my covers, whenever he wanted to be, eating whatever he wanted to eat, barking whenever he wanted to bark, and now because he didn't have Tigger and Sting to contend with, Matrix was the king. And then, there was Faith.

I was sitting there, minding my own business on January 21, 2003, because that is what I always do, and my son came into the house with that "look" on his face. We had moved again because we had obtained full custody by this time, and we had managed to rent a little house without having to put up much of a deposit. Reuben knew the rules, we couldn't have pets. The fact that we had pets, notwithstanding, Reuben knew the rules. He was standing in front of me. He was smiling. He wasn't going to tell me why, but I knew that in the 17 years I had known him that there were very few reasons for this particular smile. Funny isn't it? I can tell which of my children has let gas in the closed car by the smell, it doesn't matter how well you've trained them, they all do it, and I find it a little disturbing that I can detect from my nostrils which of my kids to blame. I'm never wrong . . . this smile, this barely showing the teeth, but all the dimples being exposed for optimal cuteness. What was he about to do? What was I about to get myself into? In a flash my life changed. "It was true Mom, Princess had a bunch of puppies and she had some of them without legs and one died because it couldn't fight off the others. Another one died when it walked into the snow and she didn't go out and get it. I found it, I buried it." A tragic story yes, but he hadn't stopped the excessive smiling. That's when it hit me. No! He didn't! He knows we can't have a dog in this house! We already broke the rules with Matrix.

Then he had to have that cat, and when one cat comes another one finds its way into my house. I was already being asked to pay more each month to cover the deposit on the animals that Frank the landlord had been so adamant about—adamant in that we couldn't have any. We had Matrix, but for some reason Frank believed me when I told him he would be staying down the street with friends. Idiot. "You didn't bring home one of those dogs Reuben!" I protested. I stomped my right foot, slammed down the dish drying towel in my hands, which I had been using to dry dishes he was suppose to have washed hours ago. "You did not bring home a puppy just because she had too many. Oh my gosh Reuben it was only two weeks ago! You can't bring a two-week old puppy here and expect it to live, its mother has to feed it, it doesn't even have its eyes open I'm sure." I continued protesting. I know I did, and there he was, smiling. While he wouldn't stop showing off those dimples, he reached into the folds of his football jersey, pulling out the fuzziest, yellowest, cutest little pointed-earred puppy I had ever seen . . . . without front legs. This was going to take a little faith!

Janet Rios (now, Martinez) is a beautiful woman, dark, Hispanic by heritage, with long, long, flowing dark hair which tends to be pulled up and bunched around her head most of the time. When she comes to my house the poor woman is subjected to torture because of her incredibly beautiful hair and pure, clean, skin. Laura and Caity have played with Janet since they were very small, perhaps as far back as their 1st and 2nd grades respectively. Janet has always tolerated them, letting them pull on her hair, making it into dozens of tiny ponytails, twisting it and braiding it. She has sat perfectly still for hours while they put makeup on her face, testing colors which probably look best on her eyebrows to be put on her lips, and vice versa. Janet is one heckuva babysitter and always has been. When the time came for Janet to graduate from high school she was honored by the vocational school she was attending when she wasn't attending Putnam City High School. Janet was the best in the State of Oklahoma in general masonry and had the mounted trowels and awards to prove it. Within a few months of her graduation Janet decided to go to college and I was her choice for an English teacher. I didn't know if she was trying to tell me that she wanted to learn something from me, or if she thought I owed her an easy A for the things my daughters have put her through all these years. Either way it was decided. I would be teaching Janet English. Toward the beginning of the Spring semester of 2003 Janet had completed her first English course and chose me again to teach her English II course, not a problem for me, but it seems to be one for her. She was making excuses the first week of school saying that she couldn't get the assignment completed because she had too much stress at home. I knew her family well, Janet and her brother Johnny had virtually lived at my house off and on since 1996, and this semester was no different. I didn't want to pry, but I explained to her that it wouldn't be fair to the other students in my class if she was excused from the first essay on Favorite Zoo Animals if they had to complete their essays on time. "I know" she complained, but it wasn't just her mother's illness, or her brother missing so much school, or her father's new girlfriend, (her parents had divorced just a few months before) and it wasn't just the fact that her sister in California wanted and needed her in that state to help with her growing family; it seems Janet had another all together interesting problem, which if I had thought about it, I would have known about because I had not seen much of her during the Christmas break. I had heard a great deal about her since Johnny, her brother, was my son's best friend, and they had been best of friends since 1996, when the two of them were in the same fourth grade class.

Janet tried to look me in the eye when she told me, but she wasn't sure I would believe her. She tried several times without being able to talk about it, and when the tears came out of her eyes I had to concede that whatever the problem was, it was serious indeed, and it was going to cause me to become involved . . . again. Normally, these things were just a matter of money, time, a little effort, whatever it took, but this seemed different. She was genuinely concerned about something she didn't have control over.

"Remember a few weeks ago when I told you my dog had puppies?"

"Yes, you told me there were some without legs and I told you they wouldn't survive, I remember."

"You said I should maybe put them down, and I was kind of laughing because I wasn't actually holding any of them."

"Yes, I thought that was funny too", I said.

"Well, Princess had a few of them without legs and Johnny found one of them dead today." I was truly sorry to hear that, it was bitterly cold outside, and I could only imagine that the puppy had gotten away from its mother. She wouldn't have gone after it, Princess was not the mothering kind.

"Janet, what's going on? ", I asked.

"I have to feed the other dogs. Princess won't do it. She won't feed the puppies."

"You're feeding the dogs yourself? You're going outside to the back lot and feeding them, with what? An eye dropper?"

"Yes! I'm using the medicine dropper that I found in the cabinet to put milk and vitamins into them. They don't always take it and I think one of them is going to die; she won't let me pick her up and Princess keeps biting me when I try. I think Princess is going to kill the dog and it's my fault." She began to cry.

"Why is it your fault?" I asked, Janet had never been able to hurt anything.

"Because, she knows I'm trying to help it, and she won't let me. It's like she doesn't want me getting close to it, but she won't help it either."

I didn't know what to tell her. I couldn't really empathize because I didn't have anything in my life to compare it to. Her dog's motherless actions were alien to me, every time one of my dogs had given birth I was there, I was the midwife, she had let me help her in every way. Princess was repelling everyone and pulling the deformed puppies underneath her in a perverse manner. It was as if she was deciding the fate of the puppies for herself; it was really getting to Janet. She couldn't let the puppies die without trying to help them. When Reuben came home from school I asked him to go by Johnny's house to check out the situation, maybe he could do something to prevent the puppies from suffering. He was, after all, a stronger person than either Janet or I when it came to possibly having to deal with putting the puppies down humanely.

Excerpts from journals:

January 28, 2003

"The word sucker is clearly painted on my pointed head or somewhere on me because it never fails to happen. I'm always caught because I don't have any common sense. I can't say no. I don't know why. Johnny and Janet (Rios) have an old dog named Princess that was supposed to be spayed a long time ago. I think I paid for that, but she wasn't spayed and naturally she had puppies. She had them last month, and now I have one. Reuben brought her to me last week. This one is extremely small, and quite odd really. Her front paw and leg are dead and the other one (right) isn't there at all, there's a little nub and a claw. It won't ever develop and she's going to be lame forever. She's sandy colored, fuzzy, smooth haired and she has a little white spot on her face near her nose. She is only going to be 20-25 pounds probably I don't know who or what the father dog is. Princess is nearly all chow, black and hairy. I guess the daddy had to be yellow and smaller. We decided to name her Faith. We could have named her Miracle because Reuben said she didn't have a chance of surviving. Maybe he just told me that, but he said that Princess was crushing her and he had to drag the puppy out from under her. I think she's going to make it, we don't let dogs die in my house, but this is going to be an experience."

January 28, 2003, (later)

Faith is drinking well, she's eating off the floor, she can't scoot up over the rim of the bowl, but that's just today. She'll get much bigger and stronger and she'll be OK. We'll definitely have to watch her to be sure she doesn't put her head in the bowl of water, she may not be able to get it out. I don't need her drowning on me. She has to be taken care of, but that's not a problem at our house. Dang it!

January 29, 2003

Faith is a really cute puppy and I probably would have picked her out if I had seen the rest of them. I don't know if they were all this badly deformed. Reu said that some were and today Johnny said that some of the puppies had died. I don't know if he's just saying that or if it is true, but Princess is a really mean dog. She may be killing the deformed puppies. I just would have thought she would have done that a long time ago.

January 30, 2003

I really miss Maurice. I didn't think I would. I didn't realize when he died a couple of weeks ago that all these feelings were going to flood back. I only met him a few times. I mean, we were friendly but we weren't really friends. Maybe we were but we weren't good friends. Why is my heart hurting? I don't get it. Laura is sick today, she has tummy cramps but I think she just wants to be home with Faith. She has her in her arms and she's telling her how she's going to get her a new skate to roll around on. Can you imagine that? Yes, Mr. Wal-Mart Man, I think his name is Barry. His son goes to school with my son. "Can we have a Barbie skate so we can cut it in half and then strap it onto our little two-legged dog? You see, she doesn't walk and she never will, her front legs are gone. (one anyway and the other useless) Faith scoots pretty good. She got under the bed and then up into her box again. Its great to see her in action really, she is determined. I'm hoping she won't even need wheels but I don't see how it would be unavoidable. I could get her a little set now and a professional one later. I have to try."

Chapter Thirteen

WHAT DID WE KNOW? We thought perhaps that Faith would have to be carted about because she didn't have any legs. It didn't dawn on us at that time that two legs in back have worked well enough for chimps in the past. Dogs aren't chimps, I know that, they aren't human either, but they do have one thing in common, well, two, they're all mammals, and they have the same Creator. I couldn't make it happen but He could. Prayer time!

Faith was going to have to get around and I was, after all, a professor at a real live college with a real live Engineering department. I can't even tell you the excitement she instilled in the hearts of the security officers when I stopped by their station first thing to let them see her, to register her as being a visitor on campus, and to let them see her scoot around. She actually left them a tiny little gift. Their reactions were precious. One of them asked me if he could frame it? I had to laugh. We used a new tissue and decided collectively not to keep it or to preserve it. Faith's ability to win hearts didn't end with me obviously, several dozens of administrators, students, teachers, and staff at Oklahoma City Community College were delighted to see her that first day we took her to find out if the students in the Mechanical Engineering classes could possibly come up with something that she could use. Anything had to be better than the half-baked Barbie skate idea, even if our little idea was created in love. I wish I had taken a picture of our poor puppy laying there on the floor trying to gnaw her way out of that contraption. To be perfectly honest, strapping Faith to the skate with velcro was not an easy task. I'm sure she wasn't wanting to be attached to it, and the skate seemed to be repelling her as well. It would roll away from us. It took two people to strap a little dog that weighed under six pounds to a Barbie skate that weighed about the same. Come to think of it, I'm glad I didn't take any early photographs of us torturing Faith, they could have been used against us in a court of law. "No your Honor, I wasn't trying to kill my dog. She's armless. Armless your Honor, Look!" Maybe I'd get off with an easy sentence.

Dr. Mansaroh was not available. His classes had started yes, and the syllabus was being followed. It was explained to me that the cause was great, but without permission from the Chair of the Department to change the syllabus guidelines, and in his case, the instructor would have to approve it as well; we would have to put the project off until the following semester. That wouldn't be until August! This was late January, and by that time the new semester rolled around my dog would be well established on her chest, or so I thought.

When I teach college students I ask them to keep a journal of everything they do from the time they come into the class to the time they leave. Their final exam is often an overview of everything as they have experienced it in class and/or at home or in their daily lives. It's no surprise to see that my journal entries during this time of my life would be helpful when recalling exactly what I was going through in terms of what I thought would be the future of this little yellow dog. Sometimes, when I have nothing else to do, I'll randomly pull out a journal, one of my hundred notebooks stashed around the house, and I'll read about a particular time in my life. Would I remember everything I wrote, would I be able to relive it if I had to? The thought occurred to me that I may have to surrender my journals for court someday . . . wow, then everyone would know exactly what I was really thinking about them. That could be interesting.

January 31, 2003

Reuben is gone. He moved out and it's sad because he's growing up but he did say that I have to feed him still. I guess the ties aren't completely cut off. He gets paid tomorrow, and I have to pay his electricity, get him groceries, and do a little with trying to get him his own phone. I'm sure I'll end up paying for that too. Wouldn't it be nice if I had a, oh, I don't know . . . a job! Oklahoma City Community College has 2 classes for me, but that's it. I lost Redlands and OBU to budget cuts. I'm not that upset about OBU, but it was money. Faith is actually pushing herself along from what I can tell. It looks like she is scooting faster, I'll say that, but she's going to have to learn to lift up that face. She bumps it to the ground with each bound and that has to hurt!

February 6, 2003

I'm an idiot. I call myself an idiot quite often, but this time I mean it. I was online and found that someone had been using my name and information for a matchmaker site. I did the unthinkable, I asked them to stop using my screen name. That set off a multitude of harassing e-mails and then it dawned on me that I'm not the only person in the world that uses that name. OK, so I guess I can mark that up to being a real dummy. Reu came by, he's not surprised I got chewed out online. He said he had a name online with several numbers behind it because there were over 400 people using the name he picked. There you go. It snowed today about 3 inches and I'm going to put Faith in it to see her reaction."

Faith not only liked the snow she dug her face into it over and over again wanting to burrow. I had to ask myself at that point if her father wasn't a yellow dachshund, but I knew better. It was nearly impossible to get her tiny face out of the snow without forcibly picking her up and moving her. She liked the feel of it, or she did until I think it dawned on her that the snow was rather cold. Her tiny furry chest and chin were completely covered and she realized about four or five minutes into the snow fight going on behind her, that she was getting a little wet. Yelp! Yelp! I looked at her and she was trying to get my attention. The crying wasn't enough to make me really think she was in any trouble, so I watched, I waited to see what she was going to do for herself. I hadn't heard her cry before. She had been completely unable to bark or make any sound whatsoever before this moment. Naming her Faith was intentional after all. We knew that God could work His miracle, but it was going to take faith to walk . . . it always does. God opened the door of the prison and He sent His Angel to guide Peter, but He instructed Peter to put on his own shoes, and to WALK out of the building itself. Walking was going to take faith. Walking was going to be Faith's work, not mine. I watched her. YELLLLP! Finally! That's what I wanted to hear, that's what I wanted to see! There she was, no longer laying on her face and chest with her head buried in the snow, the puppy was up on her hunches, sitting. Just sitting and just crying out. Something she had not done before because her mother had laid too long on her voice box. These were the first cries we had heard from our little furry baby. It was time to do the dance.

Matrix wasn't exactly the best mate for Faith. He was after all fully grown, dominant, and well . . . he's half dachshund. Dachshund have a long standing reputation of being neurotic and my black mutt was no different. It was really funny to watch him when he spotted a squirrel in the yard. The beagle in him told him to stand and point, the dachshund in him told him to dig in with all four feet about 3 inches from the ground and tear off after it. The dog literally stutters in a run-stop motion across the first 15-20 feet of the pursuit, giving the animal a heads up! Don't be scared little guy, he wouldn't know what to do if he were to catch you, the cats trained him. He would no doubt meow, and bat you away with his front paw or something. Perhaps ignore you completely.

Journal Entry:

February 9, 2003

Happy Birthday Joseph Hamilton. What a grim day for weather. I guess if you're a duck this sort of thing is good. Today at 6:00 p.m. I saw an ad in the daily on the internet and I couldn't believe it. Corgi puppies, full blood for $150.00. I can't possibly do that. I know I don't have a job. I don't have permission from my landlord for the animals that I have, why on Earth did I drive to Newcastle, Oklahoma to pick up a little tri-colored dog? For Faith. Happy early Valentine's little girl. How many other dogs can say that they got their own best friend for Valentine's Day? Getting to the place was so scary. We drove through pea soup fog from Southwest 74th off the highway all the way into Newcastle, and people passed us as if they could! I was going the speed limit and I couldn't see two feet in front of me. These people had their high beams on, a big no-no in the first place, and driving more than 70 mph in those conditions, I was going 30 by the time I arrived in Newcastle. I got lost two times and there was a man and his dog Sam to help us. "Over that way in the trailer." That was good news. We were going to a trailer in the middle of a muddy lawn, we had to walk in 30 degree weather about two city blocks from the road, no, the deserted road, to find the little beaten up trailer. For a damn dog! Well, it was a Corgi, and he was really really cute. Caity named him Ean, you pronounce it Ine. Like Mine, without the M."

By her 10th week on Earth Faith was sitting up and just about hopping to me. She would certainly think about it. If nothing else, she was at least off of her face most of the time. I wasn't sure, but there was a time that I actually thought I caught her doing deep knee squats. Reuben was doing them in front of her, and she was either trying to imitate him, or she was trying to jump up to him, but over and over again, she was making the very motions he was. That had to have played a part in building up those legs. People see Faith and just after their initial shock when they realize she doesn't have front legs, they comment on her back ones. "Wow! What leg muscles!" I suppose it's been a while for me now, and to be honest I'm very used to seeing her walking around the house and yard. I don't even notice any longer, but yes, her leg muscles are quite defined. The beginning movements were of course recorded. We have still shots and motion video clips of her first hops. Parents dream of the moments their babies walk, and they take out the camcorders to capture their every movement. We were no different. I don't think I've seen video of other puppies taking their first hops and skips, but we have Faith on tape. She made her way around the house and over a spoon first. She was trying to lick the peanut butter off of it. We had first used this method in the snow that first night. We took a little plastic spoon with peanut butter and held it just before her nose. Hop. We did it again. Hop. The dog was definitely a dog. The practice was repeated over and over again until her mind took over and the matter of being legless was forgotten. Over and over she hopped to us, and we began to think that walking would not be a far fetched idea. Placing our hands under her and moving slowly backward . . . one hand under her and the other holding a peanut butter laden spoon . . . . faith! She walks. Soon she would be making her way into the hearts of not only disabled people, but people with disabled pets. Amazingly, we received letters from local people who had seen us walking around the block, going to the stores, the vet's, or just anywhere. They had to be a part of Faith's adventure, and we welcomed their cards and invitations of hope because it meant that we as a family had actually followed our hearts and made the right decision to keep our little fuzzy girl.

The camera became her constant admirer. She didn't quite understand why we would be so interested, after all, she had to get around some day right? Peanut butter, ham, olives, grapes, tomatoes, it didn't matter. Feed the puppy and she would follow you anywhere. I remember walking into the bedroom one night when she was about 12 weeks old and catching her climbing on top of Ean to get to the top of the bed because I had left a spoonful of peanut butter in the center of it on a plate. Could she find a way? Oh yes, she found a way, Ean suffered a little, but she was most grateful. Not grateful enough to share, mind you, but she was nevertheless on top of the world. We have pictures. One of the more desperate moments involving movements came early on in Faith's life when Reuben, Laura, and Caity decided that a skateboard would be really useful. Because Wal-Mart is the only store we shop at for these sorts of things the kids took Faith into the toy department of the newly opened Super Center on N.W. Expressway. Back to Barry at Wal-Mart. He was so excited to be a part of Faith's experiences with learning to get from point A to point B. He took the kids and Faith to the area where skateboards are sold and they decided that a mini board would be best. About six dollars later, they were on their way to training poor Faith to be a master at rolling. Flop! She would not stay positioned. She should have learned. Velcro wasn't going to be a part of this torture. Shoe strings hold more things in place than simply the sides of one's tennis shoes. If I were a sadist I would have taken pictures of these sort of inventions as well, the only pictures of Faith riding on a skateboard are ASACP approved. Not that the memories aren't vivid.

Journal Entry:

March 6, 2003

Faith looks so pathetic. She's being strapped down to the skateboard the kids bought at Wal-Mart.

How did they think she was going to stay on? They put shoe strings around the board and tied her down in about 4 places. I swear, the poor dog is going to have nightmares of falling of a cliff strapped to a surfboard or something. AAAHHHGGGHH. Kids. She's going to have to walk, there's just no other way out of it. The dog's going to be killed with these contraptions."

I went on the internet and looked for sites using Google. I think my keywords were "wheels for dogs without legs" or something. I found a site at *www.wheelchairsfordogs.com* and for the next few days corresponded with them about Faith's needs. I needed to download a couple of pictures of her, take her measurements and be prepared for their responses, however, they never wrote back after I asked them to give me a price for a wheelchair or cart that Faith could use. Back to the internet and I found another site, this one was *www.dogswithdisabilities.com*. They were a bit more responsive. They told me they could not help me. I asked why of course, and without hesitation they returned my e-mail with the fact that they had never heard of a dog surviving without both of their front legs. One maybe, but the front legs, as it was explained to me, are used to push, not pull. A dog without his or her back legs can pull a cart around and get from one place to the other as long as the terrain is smooth. To expect a dog to push a cart would require strength in the entire body. The legs of course would have to be strong, the spine would be compromised, and the idea of building one unit for this one dog was simply not feasible. At least they wrote back. I thanked them. After about four weeks I received an e-mail from the people at Wheelchairs for Dogs. They had also contacted Dogs with Disabilities and were told the same thing. I suppose the idea must have created a stir in their minds, and the fact that they hadn't returned my e-mail was not to be taken negatively after all. People respond in different ways.

Faith's ability to stay put on a skateboard has not improved. She sees one now and noses it before she comes near it. She won't hop onto one, and if placed on one she runs away. Yes, runs. She developed a method of movement which far surpassed our imagination. Her ability to stand up and take off is not credited to any sort of contraption whatsoever. I recorded it diligently in my journal, and if I hadn't been there to see it for myself, I may not have believed it.

Journal Entry:

March 22, 2003

Happy Birthday Baby Boy! You got something today that you may never have realized would be a wonderful gift. Faith stood up and ran across the yard. She literally stood up and chased Ean clear across the yard when he bit her legs and then took her bone away from her. I thought she was going to kill him. I took pictures."

Ean did it! Viva la Valentines! The puppies were outside in the bright sun shinny day playing with their new rawhide bones and barking at one another. Ean, who we often call Corgus decided that it was time to test out those herding skills that are naturally inbred into his genetic makeup. He thought about it, then pounced on Faith, jumping from her left side to her right, forcing her to move from one point of the yard to the other. He had her in his control, and she wasn't the least bit happy about it. NO ONE takes the bone from this dog, or pushes her away from her food, NO ONE. Not even her own present.

Hard and fast Faith stood up completely on her back legs like a Tyrannosaurus Rex, running one foot in front of the other at a pace fast enough to be amazed at. She reached the thief and bit the head of the Corgi dog hard enough to shock the surprise right out of him. Gripping the bone in his mouth he took off and tried to escape her wrath. Nothing doing. Faith took one giant hop and then another, before long she was bounding like a kangaroo across the backyard in all her glory. This continued until the dogs met in a pile of flying fur. I think Ean was laughing at his friend, but I could hear Faith and it didn't sound very pleasant from where I was standing. Within a few seconds the little dog had given up his prize to the more dominant and certainly more bipedal animal in the backyard. Faith, the avenger! Bone retrieved, Faith laid down and continued her blissful pursuit of her rawhide. All the while Matrix, in his kingly way watched, never offering assistance to either of his subordinates.

From scooting to sitting, sitting to hopping, hopping to bounding, and finally a means of movement which still stuns and amazes everyone who sees her walking, Faith has developed into what we believe, is the ONLY upright walking biped canine in the world today. Again, as I walk her or see her rounding a corner in the house I am not impressed, I have no reaction of surprise on my face when I take her to Petsmart or to her vet's office. I'm used to seeing her walking and it is merely something that she does to get, as I mentioned, from point A to point B. She commands attention from nearly every other person and animal alive when she is noticed. To be honest, I am proud of her, and when I do see the attention she is receiving from her abilities to walk upright I am immediately reminded of her struggle, and of her self imposed determination to stand and walk. Faith comes in many ways, and certainly this dog's faith is not to be dismissed. No where is it written that animals cannot seek the Lord's will the same as we do. We may not understand their method of communication with Him but there is no reason for me to believe that He has limited His personal divine intervention to humans only. I won't ever believe that. When Faith came to us she was without the use of her arms and she was voiceless. It was an act of utter dependence on her part to be in our charge. We literally had to pick her up, put her places, help her, watch her, and make determinations for her because she could not let us know vocally that she needed out, wanted food, or simply that she wanted to be picked up. She used her eyes, her facial expressions, body language, and other methods to let us know.

It wasn't long after we took Faith into our hearts that I understood that God's love is really quite the same for us. On a larger scale of course, but when I was going through the custody battles, the divorce issues, and the financial troubles after I lost my jobs, I had felt armless in court. The long arms of the law were completely wrapped around the judge, and my voice was quieted a number of times as I stood before a seemingly heartless group of people telling me that I was unimportant, that my children were better off with people who I knew were hurting them. I was unable to make my points in that courtroom I was forced to cry, to show expression, to wait, and to depend on the only one that would forever be able to make the difference in our lives. I had to wait on God. Faith wasn't the easiest thing to have in those days and for our little dog, faith wasn't the easiest thing to demonstrate as she wound up sloshing in her own squalor when we weren't paying the best of attention.

The similarities between her physical condition and my emotional condition were parallel in so many ways. Her eyes were open as she would stare up at us and hope. My heart wanted to hear the words of peace, and I would stare, hoping that finally the judge would understand. Speaking, barking in her courtroom would only bring about disaster, as I had proved to myself over and over again. I really do have a thick head at times. If only I could be more like my son Reuben, who takes the answer he is given and walks away, thinking of another way to achieve his goals. Or maybe I could be more like my daughter Laura, who takes the answer she is given and analyzes it to the point of finally understanding it. She can justify just about anything and make her condition more acceptable. Not me, I'm exactly like Caity, what is mine is mine, if I'm right, I'm 100% right! I shouldn't be punished because someone else is too stupid to see things my way, and God help the person who dares to mess with me when I get my mind settled on something. These tactics don't really work in the courtroom and it took me just a little longer than most to figure that out. With faith came the patience I had to find, and once it was crammed down my throat by my all-to-fabulous attorney Anita F. Sanders, I was able to walk upright and run to my rawhide . . . well, to my children. And yes, I will admit, I stood upright like a Tyrannosaurus Rex and bit the heads of the people who had taken them from me. There were many parallels, including the joy on our faces when we realized that we actually can do what we think we can do if we just let go and let it happen in due time. His time, with a little faith.

Chapter Fourteen

Around the same time that Faith began to walk the United States had declared war on Iraq. I was working a temporary position at a downtown law office and I remember being in the lunch room/conference room, eating my grapes and cottage cheese, listening to the lawyers discussing the events of the day. When I put my two cents worth in I was asked to remain quiet. I couldn't believe the rudeness of these people, did they really think that because they held law degrees they had more to contribute to the conversation? Oh, wait, maybe it was because I wasn't one of them, I wasn't employed full time. I was a peon, a nobody, a . . . temporary. I was in the room before them, and it had in fact been me who had filled them in on all of the CNN and MSNBC updates. "You can go back to work now", stated a particularly egomaniac. "I'll go to work when my lunch is over," I retorted. Is it hard to see why I don't exactly keep jobs very long when working for someone else? Mr. Moler would never in a million years have been so arrogant. Within a few seconds of the eye-to-eye I-am-not-about-to-back-off standoff that was taking place in the little room, a former student of mine walked into the lunchroom. "Professor!" she cried out. "What are you doing here?" I was somewhat embarrassed to admit that because of budgetary cuts I had been released at Oklahoma Baptist University and I would not be returning until possibly in the fall. The word "professor" brought an all together different facial expression to the man sitting across the large mahogany table from me. *"Professor* Stringfellow? What do you profess?" He wanted to know.

"English for one, and Ethics, if you think you'd like to learn a little something." "Oh, funny, one would think an English teacher could be employed these days", he continued, eating his tuna salad, and smugly laughing that he had at least chosen the right path in life. I secretly wondered how his essays fared in his freshmen and sophomore years. I had somewhat of an ideas as it was my duty to clean up his letters and pleadings, at least on a temporary basis.

I had taken a few pictures of Faith with me to work that day and was actively showing them around when the arrogant lawyer from the lunch room sidled up to my desk. "Working hard?" he wanted to tease with a pointed edge. "I wouldn't have to work as hard as I do if you could spell, or use the English language in the manner that it was properly created." I came back magnificently, I thought. "You're fired! Go home immediately", was all he could come back with. In my mind I thought about using the word "twit", but chose rather to push a picture in his direction and state without being the least bit upset that the dog that I resided with would provide better company than the dog I was looking at now. One of the secretaries begged the idiot to let me stay. She was too accustomed to working out his horrid use of grammar, and knew I was the only one strong enough to stand up also to his sexual based innuendos. I don't put up with sexual harassment in the work place, how could I if I were to be successful at teaching Ethics the following semester to people I had hoped would be bright enough to listen? Her request fell on deaf ears; however, within the next few months the man was apologetic enough.

Riding on an airplane to New York City to film the Ricki Lake Show in October of 2003, I was actually given the seats across the aisle from Mr. Lunchroom Moron. His company had not seen fit to fly him First Class. We were in the bulkhead just behind First Class, where our real seats were, but we had given them up so that Faith could have more room. Faith preferred to ride in comfort, where she could lay down if necessary. Stunned and amazed to see that I told the truth about having a dog with only two back legs, the lawyer asked me to forgive his comments and for having fired me. Not a problem I said, but you know what, it was a problem. I didn't have any money coming in for several more weeks. We ate less, I paid bills late, and the war raged on, making it impossible for me to be hired. No one was interested in interviewing anyone, no one knew what was going to happen to the country. We didn't know who was going to be going to fight, we didn't know if we were to expect another 9/11, or if we were going to go in with both barrels leveled at Iraq. "That's OK, I found other work, I always do." I commented, looking down at Faith.

"Didn't she have another leg?" He asked

"Yes, it was removed in July, it had began to atrophy." I commented

"I read where you changed vets. Did the first one think it needed to stay on?"

"No, she was a great vet. She didn't want to talk to the media." I answered.

With Faith being featured on *Ripley's Believe it or Not, CNN, MSNBC*, and in national and international magazines, Dr. Delbridge chose not to discuss the condition of her patient. Faith was more than just a patient actually, the world was interested in her progress. I switched vets when I found Dr. Hartford. He was good, he was close, he was willing to answer questions. I added that I thought the new vet was cuter than Dr. Delbridge too, but you have to understand, he's a guy, and I went to school with

Diane Delbridge when we were just little kids. She was the first and only choice for me when it came to helping me and my little dog. She's the best vet on the planet if you ask me.

"Cute matters I guess." He laughed, and I suppose our old battle of the stubborns had to be put aside. Dammit. This guy was actually a nice man and he seemed interested in my little puppy. I can't ever hold grudges . . . . God's mean to me that way. Just as I find a really good grudge and get going on it, He breaks my stride, softens me up and there I am forgiving people. My son does rub off on me after all. Laura would continue the grudge, but she would categorize it, place a value on it, and make appropriate accommodations for any future responses to the individual. Caity forgives everyone, but she never forgets. Once burned Caity will forever dismiss. Forgiveness must take a bit of faith as well, as I have found out that it really does feel good to have the peace that comes from letting go of the feelings I held against someone. But just a little grudge now and then, that wouldn't be too bad, would it?

Chapter Fifteen

At the close of spring 2003 I had heard enough about war when I turned on my television set. I was about up to my eyeballs in financial problems, having not been hired by anyone with an the slightest idea of what it cost to live these days and to raise a family. I was sinking a little too deeply in my own self pity about being overweight, and there wasn't much to look forward to either. Something had to give. Somehow, someway, I had to find a way to smile again and that's when the idea hit me: I called the CBS local news station KWTV-Channel 9 because my best friend Jeannie's husband had worked there at one point and I remember him telling me that news anchor Kelly Ogle (another cute man) simply loved feel-good stories about family oriented things. Family, church, morality, good things to put into the news because quite frankly, the world had proved to be a pretty nasty place. Anytime Kelly could come up with a little story about something really cool, he was going to show it, and make the biggest effort to spread the joy. Kelly was out the day I called, and whoever it was that answered the phone at KWTV didn't feel it necessary to pass along my little tale about a two-legged dog in Oklahoma City that walks upright and leaves everyone smiling in her wake. Linda Cavanaugh, however, at the NBC news station of KFOR-TV channel 4 was in. She, like Kelly, is a prominent, wonderful anchor with many years of experience, grace and charm. She wanted to do the story on Faith, and she wanted to do it that night! Sorry Kelly, I tried.

Linda sent out a cameraman to my house to pick up a few shots, maybe of the dog running around the yard with the kids, maybe taking a stroll down the street. This couldn't be a very big piece, she knew just where it was going to be placed in that evening's news and the story needed to be written on the QT as it was already getting close to 5:00 p.m. When Dennis Anderson came to the house what he saw was anything but usual. We were there, smiling of course, waiting to greet him, to shake his hand, and to introduce him to our furry buddy. He got on his cell phone and called the station with news about Faith being remarkably unusual. He had thought in his mind, he confessed, that Faith walked on her front legs, dragging her rump in the air somehow. He admitted that seeing her walking upright was more than just a little surprising. He stayed quite a while filming and asked me if he could come back if he needed more footage. Sure, why not, this is the sort of thing I think Faith was made to do. She was created to be the smiling, laughing dog without a care in the world. Go ahead Mr. Cameraman . . . shoot away! Come back tomorrow, the next day, and any other day if it makes the people giggle or gives them hope that they can do more than they first thought they might be able to do.

We didn't really interview with KFOR that day. Laura told the camera a few things about Faith; the fact that she is terribly spoiled, that she eats too much, we take her for walks, and then there was a little blurb about thanking God that she was in our lives. It was barely noticeable on tape when the story aired but it stood out on its own somehow. People have commented several times about Laura giving God the credit for making Faith and/or giving her to us.

"Now Faith is an ordinary dog, she chases the cats with the best of them." Linda concluded in the story on the night of June 23, 2003. Within hours KFOR called me to see if they could run the story over the Associated Press. Why not? Again, I thought that if someone out there in the big, bad world could use a smile, it may as well come from the story about our puppy. She was laughing, laying by my side when the phone rang and I gave my permission for the story to be shot across the world instantly. Within a few more hours the people of Germany, Sweden, England, Holland, and France had called me. I was literally on the phone from 4:03 a.m. to 9:14 a.m. Central Standard Time, talking to news people all over the world. Laura gave an impromptu interview to a London based radio station, and agreed to be called later that afternoon to be live on a particular show that details stories with strange and bizarre twists. Stories the world finds both odd and fantastic at the same time. Pictures of my daughter Laura and my dog appeared on the covers of tabloids within days. I was called by the editor of the *National Enquirer* as he wanted to run a feature story about her. My mind raced as I suddenly imagined Martians from outer space wearing Faith-costumes, landing in the desert and demanding to be taken to Pamela Anderson. Nothing was going to be out of place I was promised. The *National Enquirer*, according to their leader, was capable of telling full truths as well as sensationalized news. I agreed to the interview and pictures being printed as long as the stories written were true, and any picture of Faith was flattering. The agreement was made and into our house came Mr. Stephen Holman, not only a resident of Tulsa, Oklahoma and a photojournalist for the Tulsa World, but he is also a contract photojournalist for the *National Enquirer, The Star, The Globe, National Geographic for Kids*, and several other major magazines. This could explain the sudden onslaught of global coverage immediately following the breaking story in the *National Enquirer*.

"LISA MARIE HAS A MELTDOWN!" read the front cover of the July 29 issue of The *National Enquirer*, and I didn't care. I had been called the day before it was released and told that Faith was on page 30. There she was! Walking and going places. Her left arm flinging around, useless, and splayed backward. Standing on her own two feet, crossing the pavement, going through the living room, playing tug of war with the other dogs, and basically just having a good time. My little dog, my daughter Laura, even Caity was in the magazine with Ean. You know what I did, I stood in line at Wal-Mart and purchased 40 copies for myself. The lady didn't have to ask me twice to explain it. She laughed out loud and picked up her PA telephone. "Ladies and Gentlemen in Wal-Mart, today on sale at every counter in the magazine racks we have the *National Enquirer* featuring one of Oklahoma City's most admired residents. Faith the two-legged dog is on page 30, come and get your copy. Her mother is buying out the store!! Hurry!" It was so cute the way my daughter blushed every time I showed another customer. She finally decided to run to the pet department and look at the fish swimming in their tanks until I was finished showing off. That took a while.

Making my way to another Wal-Mart just down the road, to every 7-11 store in the area, and to a few bookstores that I knew carried the *National Enquirer*, I continued to embarrass Laura over and over again.

Caity didn't mind at all, she wasn't the least bit concerned about the coverage because there wasn't a picture of her baby belly fat plastered on the subsequent pictures. Could they have chosen a less flattering picture of Laura? Perhaps, but at least they chose others where she is smiling and looking more attractive. It's just that every time we see that particular first photo showing up on the internet, in other tabloids, on news stations across the nation, and in magazines we didn't have communication with, Laura is quick to point out that she really isn't that fat. That the belly pooching out is just a fluke, which it was of course. Faith looks good, and that was a plus for us all. Proud parents we were, our little doggy was making it big and all because she had the guts to stand up to the world with a little faith of her own.

Laura and I decided that because of all of her efforts, Linda Cavanaugh and the rest of the great people working for KFOR-TV needed to meet Faith in person, or in dog. We drove her to the station and she was immediately recognized. We were allowed into the lobby of the station during a time that news was being written but not necessarily broadcast. Tammy Payne and Lance West were just about to go on camera for the 5:00 p.m. show, but they had time to do a little hugging before they went on the air. I remember a page doing a little clean up duty around Tammy as she tried to remove a few dog hairs that she managed to collect in the petting process. Linda

Cavanaugh couldn't have been more beautiful. She graciously allowed us to go backstage, to walk around the news room meeting literally every employee at KFOR-TV. One in particular, Ali Meyer ran up and coming news anchor who, like Linda, is tall, thin, well mannered and loves dogs. She plopped down immediately to Faith's level and began giving her kisses. I thought to myself, this must be a fairly cool place to work if people come and go wearing great looking clothes from the waist up, and are able to report on the good and the bad of the world. Trophies were everywhere, indicating that the news, weather, and sports had all been given a great deal of recognition not only in the state, but from across the nation and the world as well for great coverage. Faith's story was just going to have to be accredited to KFOR-TV, it was Linda Cavanaugh who had the foresight to put it on the air and it paid off in more ways than one.

While Laura and I were at KFOR-TV, a phone call came into the newsroom. Had I not been there to see it happen I might not have believed it. One of the guys answering the news desk phone told Gunnar, one of the best producers in the building, that *I* had a phone call from *Ripley's Believe it or Not*. They were calling me at the new station. I never did find out if they had called my house first and perhaps Caity had told them where I was that afternoon. I took the call, and within a week I was hosting a blond, young, female producer named Jeannie for the internationally well known show *Ripley's Believe it or Not*. She and her crew wanted to film a day in the life of the now famous two-legged dog. What we filmed was anything but the typical day in the life of our dog. What a boring show that would be: getting up from the bed to go pee, play with the other dogs, coming back to bed, eating a little here and there, chasing the cats, going back to bed, and maybe making a visit to the neighborhood grocery store or Petsmart if we were feeling particularly outgoing. What we filmed was a day in the life of a movie star perhaps but not my dog. They had us setting up staged scenes of breakfast, bringing friends over to talk, going to the park to chase geese, taking a trip to the ball park where Faith was admired by hundreds of spectators. Next we went downtown to Oklahoma City's more prestigious tourist attraction Bricktown. While walking the canal, taking a boat ride, doing the in and out game of every eating establishment, watching people fly out of the restaurants to see her, we enjoyed the faces and the expressions of people who for the first time saw her walking on her back legs . . . . like a human. The entire process took over 10 hours to film, and needless to say, after the filming, dog and owners were exhausted.

During one of the segments a group of mentally challenged people were visiting the city from out of state, they were so happy to get a chance to pet Faith, but the editing floor holds more important moments than we will ever imagine I suppose. It would have been great to have more shots of Faith visiting with people who are so overwhelmed by her that they laugh and cry at the same time. For these people, and their caregivers, Faith represents hope and the ability to give from inside of yourself when you think you can't go any further. There was a few seconds in the telecast where Faith is meeting with a young blind boy. Because the boy and his family did not speak English, it was difficult to translate their excitement for the chance meeting; however, facial expressions and laughter again were the tools of faith, showing the nation, and the world, that with just a little hope and a little faith in ourselves as well as what may be waiting for us just outside a downtown restaurant, we can make life a little happier when we believe that we can make it a better place. These are the moments I believe I have forgotten all the loss in my life. In the middle of a crowd of people who are hugging and petting my little dog, I forget that I was saddened by the death of my friend earlier in the year. Perhaps it is his spirit that comes out when Faith is being so happy.

I recall a time on stage in August of 1979, that he looked as if he were wagging his tongue in complete elation! Maybe it was my imagination, but there did seem to be a correlation between the events of my life and the introduction of our dog Faith. More than once I have had to ask myself if God hadn't sent down an Angel in order to bring about my joy which I had somehow misplaced. Why not use a little legless dog to show the world that anything is possible? I couldn't imagine there being a less likely hero. "Sometimes", as Linda Cavanaugh reported "these stories can leave you scratching your head in wonder!" Was she ever right.

After Ripley's aired my phone wouldn't stop ringing. It wasn't always someone from another state or country wanting to talk to Faith, or to do a show about her. We had calls from German TV shows and Switzerland, the Germans came out to do a story and filmed us in our day-to-day lifestyle, much like the *Ripley's* people had done. We were under an exclusivity contract with *Ripley's* until their show ran, and the German producers guaranteed me that they too would wait to air their show. The *Oklahoma Educational Television Association* (OETA) of Tulsa came out to do a show. Their taping was only about four hours, and to be honest, I liked it a little better than I did the *Ripley's* coverage if only owing to strange camera angles and tricks of the trade using fading and whatnot. OETA's show was clean, pure, and to the point. Royal Ailes, a rather innovative producer, if I may say so, was a bit more understanding of my goals for Faith, and was quick to use video, home movies, still shots and interviews for his production.

The OETA coverage aired the same month as did *Ripley's*, but for a more local audience. Using the growing resume my dog was accumulating I decided to contact a few car dealers in the area to see if they would be interested in loaning me a good new vehicle to drive Faith around in so we could get to the hospitals, children's homes, and other places I believe in my heart she is actually suppose to be visiting. I would love to be full time employed as my dog's chauffeur, taking her to places where the sad and lonely can actually be made happy, but this avenue I was taking didn't seem to be getting me anywhere. It didn't matter to any of the local dealers if Faith was able to walk upright, or walk up stairs for that matter, her owner, me, wasn't solvent enough to afford the payments on a new car. Didn't I mention I wanted them to loan it to me? I thought it would be good publicity for them and good transportation for me. This idea, to date, has not caught on. I am unable financially to do what I believe Faith was made for because I simply do not have the financial means to do it. I can't take off work and travel to the hospitals outside of our city, I can't take off work and go to the area homes either if I am expected to work and pay bills. This is one more area in my life that I believe will be handled in time, with a little faith on my part.

After the *National Enquirer* and before *Ripley's* came out I got a call from Margaret Dunbar of Big Dogs Sports. Big Dogs is a fantastic clothes line of sportswear with hoodies, tee-shirts, fleece, gear, and so much more. They have a website at *www.bigdogs.com* and anyone who isn't familiar with Big Dogs can go and see for themselves the fun line up of clothes items available. The logo on the Big Dog lines is a black and white St. Bernard, sometimes it is a girl dog, and sometimes it is a boy dog, but it is always big, strong, and I couldn't help but notice, a four-legged dog. When Margaret called me with an offer to make Faith an honorary Big Dog I had to let her in on the not-too-secret secret that Faith actually only weighs 26 pounds. She isn't the least bit BIG in terms of size. This news wasn't news to Margaret, a fan of Faith's. She had seen her on the pages of *National Enquirer* and had read about her extensively on the internet where her growing list of sites and credits was becoming incredible. I couldn't believe people were interested in chat rooms dedicated to my dog and her condition. Margaret wanted to send us a few things, gifts, toys, collars, etc. She wanted to know if there was anything she could do to help Faith as she saw Faith's "Paws-ative" attitude toward life. I told her I would let her know. *Ripley's* and Dunbar had talked about product placement during the *Ripley's* show, but alas that didn't happen. Ricki Lake didn't mind allowing me to hold a Big Dog squeaky-toy the day we interviewed with her on her show about the very best of Ripley's for the year 2003. It was amazing, as we flew to New York City with Faith in the seat next to me, not under the plane with the cargo I had to stop for a second somewhere over the Great Lakes and think to myself that I would never in a million years think that I would be going to New York to be on a show to talk about my dog, even if that dog was the most amazing animal on the planet. American Airlines deserves a lot of credit for allowing Faith to fly up in the cabin with me, and not in the cargo with other animals. Recognizing Faith as a celebrity they have an entire paragraph dedicated to this in their flight manuals. You can imagine the looks on the faces of the other passengers as we pass through security wherever we go, through the boarding area, and onto the planes. Whenever we fly, we fly American. I can't say enough about the traveling comforts this airline has brought to myself, my family, and of course, to my dog.

Chapter Sixteen

On that first flight to New York we were waiting in the airport in Oklahoma City when Laura noticed a group of soldiers coming in from a flight that had just arrived. She wanted to introduce Faith to them because they may have been in Iraq, they were certainly America's finest, and she just wanted to say hello and thank them for their dutiful service. One of the guys, a private that was probably in his late teens looked at Faith and pulled out his cell phone. "Commander!" he shouted, "That dog we saw in the magazine in Kuwait is standing right in front of me!" I was just as shocked at hearing this as I'm sure he was at seeing Faith. He bent down to pet her, and all of the soldiers began calling people, taking pictures with the cell phones and cameras to show everyone they knew back at their base camp in Kuwait that they were greeted at the airport by the two legged dog. A brave and handsome soldier with an arm wrapped in a military sling asked if I could pick Faith up so he could pet her. Seemed he had shrapnel in his leg as well and he couldn't bend very well. I thought my eyes wouldn't stop pouring out tears. Here he was, asking me if I could trouble myself to lift 26 pounds of a little dog and he had been on the front line obviously, he had fought for me, he had given up part of his body, and I was much more than thankful to him for it. I told him I would salute every soldier I would ever come in contact with because it meant so much more to me now. So much more.

I picked my dog up, and I held her out to him. I heard it first, then I saw it. Hundreds of people in the airport were standing and giving these guys an ovation for their bravery, their work, their courage to be where they were, and for doing what they were ordered to do. The first private we met looked up and he saluted the crowd. I only thought I had tears in my eyes when I lifted up Faith to the wounded man, now I knew I did, but I didn't care.

One of the times we flew back from New York, and I think it was the first time; we flew through Chicago O'Hare Airport to get to New York, but through the St. Louis Airport coming back. What a joyous smile Faith put on her face when she encountered the moving sidewalks in St. Louis. If you ever get a chance to play on the moving sidewalks please do. Oklahoma City needs to install a few of these things if for no other reason but to give me something to do with Faith on afternoons when we get a little bored. If I lived near the St. Louis airport I would take Faith as often as possible. That little dog can fly when she gets aboard these things. She won't stop running. It is the funniest thing in the world to watch, but to realize the expressions and the looks of utter amazement on the faces of the people both on the moving sidewalk we're on, and the ones opposite to us, to see Faith running as if in place, going a million miles a minute, bent over to balance herself, and racing me to the other end. She nearly pulls off her collar each time we get on one. The only thing more fun than the moving side walks may be the concrete paths of Central Park or the streets of Times Square at night.

Getting to NYC to do these shows wasn't easy. It sounds good doesn't it? You get a call from a nationally syndicated show, they want you to be on their show, and you go, you get paid, and all of the sudden you're talking to famous people, doing what the famous people do, going where they go. Well, in the years I spent working in Hollywood in the 1980's there were a few things I learned about the "famous" so to speak. Not much of what I knew about them was of much interest to me; however, my daughter Laura was excited, thinking perhaps she would be meeting Rupert Grint, the good looking red-headed boy who plays Ronald Weasley of the Harry Potter fame. Why he would magically appear in NYC at the same time she was there is beyond me, but I never rain on my girl's dream.

Journal Entry

October 27, 2003

9:30 p.m. 24 hours from now I'll be in my hotel with Laura. Ricki's people said they didn't have enough money in their budget to bring Caity along with us. I don't see why not. They had enough to give me $400 for missing work. It would mean one more ticket, we could use the same money to eat on, and the hotel room would be shared. They just didn't want to let her come I suppose. I have had such a bad time of it with these people. They want too much. First it was Laura's birth certificate, a note from her father, which of course I explained to them we don't do notes from him, we don't even talk to him. They wanted him to say it was OK for her to be on TV. I faxed them the orders from July 27, 2001, explaining that I had sole and full custody. That was enough, but then they wanted proof of her name being Stringfellow. It isn't Stringfellow, it's Stickley, but Toby Keith's real name isn't Toby Keith now is it? She goes by Laura Stringfellow. We listed her as Stickley on the plane for their manifest, but she will be called Laura Stringfellow from anyone addressing her, and that, is by her request not mine. I had to have her birth certificate, a social security card, which wasn't a problem, but please! Next thing you know the airlines will require a rechargable Starbuck's card to get on board. Faith has to bring her vet's notes saying she is free of disease and disorders, that can't happen. She has a major disorder, hello, she doesn't have front legs. It's OK, I think they just want proof that she has had her shots and a statement that proves she doesn't have worms or something. No muzzle was being required on the plane, and that was good news. We were able to walk right on the plane, and that really is something to see.

Before the news story about Faith's abilities to walk upright I had a few other things going on in my life which required more than just a little faith to get me through. Because I'm a professor of English, and not employed full time at any one university, I was asked to take a summertime job selling insurance for a company called Conseco. It is true that Conseco had been in the news recently regarding their own financial difficulties of which I had absolutely no idea about; I was being hired to go door-to-door in small towns and communities on the west side of Oklahoma, literally trying to find people willing to buy cancer policies. I had no intention of keeping the position for any longer than I needed to, but the fact is, I really enjoyed my work. There were elements of it of course, that weren't conducive to feeling secure, for instance I was living in tiny hotel rooms in towns I had never heard of. There was the element of surprise

when and if some good ol' boy with a key from last
month's visit may be waltzing in on me, which
happened when I was taking a shower. Thank God
he was polite enough to apologize and leave the room.
My job required a great deal of leg work on my part
and a daily schedule of working at just after dawn to
just after dark, which in the middle of June is usually
after 9:30 p.m. The hours were long, the work tiring,
and because I was driving alone most of the time, I
was completely on my own when it came to needing
my car towed into town from out in the booneys, to
having my tire pop out from under me out in the
middle of nowhere. That's not true exactly, I was in
the middle of the countryside just outside of Fargo,
Oklahoma, which is just North and East of Gage,
and its just North of Arnett, so it wasn't like I was
nowhere, I was in the dustiest, loneliest, most isolated
area of the greater western section of our great state,
but at least I had the prairie dogs, lizards, snakes,
deer, and LeRoy "Chuck" Bailey to help me. Like
Chuck, Fargo is a loner. Not much going on in Fargo
any day of the year, and any year of the decade. Chuck
was a member of the "Liars Club", which is a group
of older gentlemen who met at the gas station (*The*
gas station) and cafe on the main road. It was up to
Chuck to keep tabs on everyone for me, because I
knew he would know where they were. I involved
him immediately, from the first day on the job when
he bought a policy from me. I don't know if he felt

sorry for me because I had never held a baby lamb before, maybe it had more to do with the fact that his beautiful wife of so many years had passed away, and our company was instrumental in getting him the benefits as soon as they were needed. Chuck was a die-hard Conseco fan and I needed one when I broke down not thirty feet away from a make shift meth lab.

"What are you doin' over there?" He called to me.

"Car broke down . . . . got a flat."

"Bound to happen. Let me help." He said.

"Is that a meth house? I smell something . . . ugly." I asked.

"Meth? Why, I don't know, maybe, probably, sure why not? It'll probably blow up like the rest of them do. If these kids that make the stuff ever took a Science class and passed it they may end up saving themselves a whole mess of trouble." That's Chuck. That's Fargo, well, that's Oklahoma period, but there is still more of an element of this behavior and feeling of genuine friendship in smaller towns around the state. After he helped me get my car going I took full advantage of him and used him for references until the day that I left the town some four weeks later. Monday through Thursday I worked Fargo, I had the entire city actually, all 580 people, and that included the 366 that lived out of the city itself. I had the opportunity, though not the pleasure, of selling insurance to the family of the biggest, fattest, strongest, and most adorable yellow Labrador I had ever seen in my life. Colonel was indeed huge, in fact, I believe someone in Fargo told me they had seen Faith on KFOR-TV and they mentioned that Ali Meyer needed to come out to Fargo to meet up with ol' Colonel. 248 pounds of yellow dog. He made my little Faith look like . . . well, a little dog.

I sold insurance for Conseco until such a time that a problem developed between what I was selling and what was being proceeded and issued. In the insurance business these numbers are never the same, but for unknown reasons my sales were not being issued, and this could only lead to one conclusion, I wasn't being paid. Looking back at it I can say without a doubt that my leaving Conseco when I did was probably one of those answered prayers that I actually felt more than verbally prayed. Bailey was great, as were all of the other members of the Liars Club; some of them have mundane lives, some not. One of my favorite members was a man I'll call Jack. Jack was a smaller man in stature, but in so many ways he reminded me of my friend who had passed away. He was bearded, about the same height and weight too, but there was something about Jack that made the light bulbs explode when he walked into a room. I saw it happen and thought immediately that he had to be producing some sort of electrical charge that he's not even aware of. "I can't keep lights in my house!" he exclaimed when I gave him a look that obviously required an answer. "I can just be standing there, maybe in the hallway or something, and if I stand there too long the lights blow." Strange, yes, but no doubt one of the more interesting facts about Fargo, Oklahoma. Jack had been many things before he retired. He had worked on the assembly lines, in the trenches digging ditches, he had driven trucks and been a rancher; today he relaxes in his home, a trailer at the edge of town and enjoys going through his scrap books (in the dimmed light of the kitchen) pouring over the many exotic places his work and play have taken him. In his living room is a large picture of him standing on top of Kilimanjaro I think.

There couldn't be a more energetic man in the world, and yet this one had been stopped physically by an accident. Still, with injuries, forced early retirement, and living in a tiny little community, Jack's smile was larger than life, much like his experiences. We had an opportunity to discuss cancer policies of course, one of which he may or may not have signed up for; but we had an opportunity to discuss Christ, faith, life after death, and issues that meant a little more to both of us. I told Jack about Maurice, how he had passed earlier in the year, and I told him that at times I could feel him in my house, even near me. Jack had that smile again, he told me that happens to him as well with a dear friend, a woman he had met on one of his excursions. They had been pen pals for a while, and after several years of contact she had stopped writing. Not being able to reach her by phone or letter he assumed the worst. Within a month or so of his feeling that she had passed away she came to visit him in a dream. He told me that she had died, and that it had been a peaceful death; that he wasn't to cry for her, or worry about her family. All things were taken care of in her life and now of course, in her after life. He had the feeling that she was telling him that they would see each other again, and to bring her point more to the surface of his heart, she told him a few names of relatives of his that had greeted her in Heaven.

Being a Believer, Jack took what she said to heart and let it go no further. This was the first time he had revealed his story. I was honored to be the one he told it to. I know he wouldn't mind me mentioning it; just thinking about what can be our driving force is remarkable. The issue of faith is so dear to you, and to me. It's private, it's public, it's hard to pin down. For me it is the feeling that I can't make it unless I give up the reins. I can't make the air that I breathe, but its still my responsibility to draw in the breath. I know that having the faith to let go of whatever the situation is and to let it work itself out is often seen as the lazy way out, but to tell you the truth, it's actually much harder to let go than one might think. For years I thought I was in control of my life, and all the things I had to do to be successful were totally up to me. Well, going through the divorce in 1997, and the subsequent battles in court over custody, child support, contempt of court charges, and so much more; I learned that I am not in control. I thought I was, but I am surely not. It became so very clear to me the day the judge ordered me not to call the police; a single act of stupidity on her part, which led to hours, days, weeks, and months of tragedy for myself and my children. If I couldn't be allowed the very basic of rights, what was I to expect? I let it go. When the same judge told me I was not going to be going to law school, even though I had been given a full ride at one of the best law schools in the southwest region of America, Oklahoma City University School of Law, I found myself buried in despair. She was literally telling me to my face that I was not allowed to go to law school and seek custody at the same time. In her opinion, not the law's opinion, going to law school would take too much time away from the children. I had a choice to make. Because the ABA, the American Bar Association, did not allow first and second year law students to work, she determined that I would be asking my ex-husband for full support. This wasn't the case, but nevertheless, she ruled and ordered me in chambers not to seek a degree in law. Not at this time, she further instructed. If I wanted to pursue one the day after Caity turned 18, then so be it. She basically admitted that she could not make this ruling in court, however, if I chose to go against her (almighty) powers, she was going to see to it that I was no longer a contender for parental guardianship.

How dare she! I stood in the corner of her office behind the courtroom. I stared at her in utter silence.

I had completed my Bachelors degree at Oklahoma City University, and had sufficient grades to mandate a full ride to a law school that she knew was the best. She knew that my years of experience as a legal assistant had led me to the decision of wanting to be a lawyer, and that I would actually someday pursue the bench; this was my destination, not her's, and her ruling was both unconstitutional and wrong. I let it go. I didn't have a choice. I let it go. For grins and giggles I applied for law school at Harvard Law about a year after the judge's ruling. I obtained a telephone interview and was told that based on my grades and writing sample I would actually be given a face-to-face interview. I thanked the proctor and declined. But it is nice to know I have the door of opportunity still available to me someday. One of the nicest things about my decision to continue with an educational path is that I now have a Masters in Literature, and am just about to complete my PhD. in Administration and Leadership. If I didn't have the credentials at the time of the offer for a face-to-face, I would surely have them now. All is not lost, there is still another tick to go on the clock, and as long as there is, there is reason to pursue the dream. I believe in chasing dreams and in doing so, I believe you may run into a judge or two, perhaps a custody battle, a bad relationship, a co-worker that won't let you breathe five seconds without reporting it to the boss, or maybe you'll run across your boss doing cocaine . . . that can set you back! I believe that letting go is so very important, and that the only way you can do it is to trust that the One you leave that trust with is capable of doing what is best for you. I love the words of the Psalmist when he wrote: "I know who I am believed, and am persuaded that He is able to keep that which I've committed, until to Him against that day". Go ahead and call me a holy-roller, it won't be true, but if it sounds like I may put too much faith in a God I haven't seen yet, it's because there really isn't another way. Fighting the fights alone makes no sense. Fighting the battles with others who feel the same that you do about faith makes far more sense. At the very least you have a network, a frame, and a gaggle of friends (are they actually called gaggles, because I know that a group of owls is called a Parliament) and you have a much better chance of regaining the confidence you need to continue the basic things you have to continue doing on a routine basis, not to mention the tough moments that come along.

PART THREE

Letting Go

Chapter Seventeen

The concept for writing this book came easily to me. The little dog that was given to us, or rather taken by my son without asking and then obtaining permission from Janet and her mother, would take more than the normal amount of love, time, effort, money, and support. We knew that. No one had to bring that bit of information to the surface. I saw her face . . . I lost my heart. It would not have mattered if she had no legs, this dog was going to be mine, and like everything else in my life, she was going to make it. She didn't really have a choice. There she was, laying in the palm of my hand, gnawing on my finger, looking up to me with the expression of both determination and a hopeful stare asking for help. She was going to make it. It would take countless hours of physical assistance yes, we were going to have to bend way over to place our hands under her, to guide and lead her across the patio concrete, the carpet, the tiled floor and the backyard grass, but she was going to make it. We were going to have to watch her to be sure she didn't fall off the couch or stumble off the stairs, get into the water bowl without being able to get her head out, or to crawl into the shower when we weren't looking. That was actually quite scary, and an experience neither she nor I will forget.

I stepped on what I thought was a loofah, but instantly the loofah squealed . . . loofahs don't squeal, and this was one of those times I lost all control and screamed out loud. No one was home and I thought I had killed the dog! Thankfully, she recovered, I recovered, and if for any reason she may have had soapy water in her lungs before I stepped on her, it had definitely been let out by the compressing of my big, fat, foot on her tiny, wet, yellow body. This dog can be under your feet, between your legs, tripping you, and generally being the biggest nuisance in the freakin' world, but something about her face and her expression let's you know that she's only doing it because she loves you.

At the time when our family was emerging from several years of battles of emotion, finance, stress, and court ordered visitation, this puppy brought to us an awareness that we are not the only reason the world turns on its axis. God allowed us to literally become the saving grace for Faith, one of His tiniest Angels. Like ourselves, when we were struggling to survive, and to balance our lives having to relearn how to cope with the simplest things life had to offer, Faith was born without the use of her arms, her voice, the love of her

mother, security, warmth, she was even neglected the
right to six weeks of nourishment before being carted off
to be the welcomed present for someone who had always
wanted a dog just like her. There are no other dogs just
like her! She may be the only two legged dog in the
world that walks upright all of the time, and even this
was not afforded to her at the time she was born. Faith
was unable to do anything without help, and we were
the ones who were being given that challenge and that
responsibility. I constantly hear people say "God bless
you for what you've done. Most people would have put
her down." I feel a bit embarrassed when they say it,
because it was my first instruction to Janet. There was
no way the dog could make it if her own mother wasn't
allowing her to live at that age. "God bless you for keeping
her, you're a Saint." Well, I don't know about that, but I
can tell you that I do believe she is one, and I bless her
on a daily basis. I think she realizes we love her, but I
don't think she has a clue of how proud we are of her.

Before someone can begin to think another person
(or owner) is proud of them, there has to be something
that the person would be proud of. Faith doesn't have
any idea that there is something wrong with her. She
knows she doesn't have legs, she figured that one out
when we went to Dolese Park during the filming of
Ripley's Believe it or Not. It had been the first time for
Faith to visit the park's lake area and we let her go to
chase the geese. We knew she didn't have legs, and
we all naturally assumed she realized it as well. Not.

The dog ran up to the geese on her back legs, which you can imagine only frightened the poor dears ever so much more than normal four-legged predators coming at them; she ran straight into the lake and didn't stop when the water went over her head! Come back, you senile animal! You don't have front legs, you can't doggy-paddle! Luckily for Faith, and I suppose everyone, Laura swims. She was out in the water in a flash, pulling her wet puppy back to safety. The initial reaction for all of us was to gasp with open mouths, but once we saw Faith's tongue hanging out, wagging and her tail thumping the air over and over, we realized that she wanted to give it another go. What a dog. There wasn't the least bit of fear in her, and she wasn't that upset to be without legs, she simply ran up to her waist in the water the second time, slow going, yes, and every duck or goose in the park spread the news rather quickly, but she had fun and she continues to have fun as often as we go. We have pictures.

Understandably, this book is an inspirational book for those, who like me, have faced difficulties and couldn't find ways to ease the pain long enough to find a little peace. It is also for those who have experienced depression and need to know that there are answers to the silent, often never expressed prayers kept so deeply inside of their hearts. I have pains in my soul from time to time too, doubts that what I'm doing is wrong, or that what I'm thinking about doing is going to be a mistake. Depression has never really been an option for me, though I think it snuck in without permission on an occasion or two. I was always too busy to recognize the symptoms. Depression to me was a state of mind and if I could just push it back with work, keeping my mind busy, my strategies going, making plans, finding new things to think about, I could effectively break the depressed feelings into pieces. This worked for a while I suppose, it wasn't until the day I was stopped and forced to give everything up (not by choice) that I realized that I had not effectively broken the feelings into pieces, I had managed to organize these feelings, and to put them into neat little piles, somewhat like Laura would do, which would someday need to be dealt with . . . but not today. That was my strategy. It was one of those denial tactics I suppose. I'll fight it off, I'll win, I'll win, I have no other options. What an idiot! I finally found peace through the assistance of helping the yellow dog in my lap. Though through our love and time she learned to grow, walk, and take the world by the tail; I learned to let go and to let the natural order of things take place.

God has not left His throne and the last time I looked, all of His twinkling stars were still aligned in their places. So then would I be realigned. I had to believe it, because it was a promise, because it was true. I've learned that I can now fully understand how the frustrations of the daily struggle, the future goals, and the needs of our families can be such an oppression. These feelings can lead someone to not only feel depressed, but to begin feeling overwhelmed, overrun and incapable of climbing out of the hole they've created for themselves, or the hole they were thrown into, which ever may be the case; but there really is a way out. With just a little faith and a lot of hard work. When we were hurting it took much more than the faith alone. Promises are good, but they do require work, work that can only be found in the hearts of the person who truly does want to make a change. Sometimes finding our own way out seems impossible and I'm all for asking or help.

My dad, because he is a normal guy, when we were growing up, would never stop and ask directions. It didn't matter how lost we were, and sometimes I think I do that with my personal life and my goals. I get stuck, I dig myself in, and even though the phone book is sitting right there, and I can ask for help for something medical, financial, emotional, physical . . . . I don't. I think it would be a total waste of time, it might cost something, it may set me back, it could be made worse if I involve someone . . . all bad excuses, but excuses I have used many times. The calm before the storm is a warning, and the calm which follows the storm, to me, is a promise that I was brought through said storm. I tend to pray a little more, and pick up the phone more often nowadays. I don't mind asking for help because I don't want the one I see in the mirror to be the one I used to be, I want to see the person I want to see. I wish I could be the person my dog thinks I am, or maybe the person these people I meet on the street think I am. They bless me, say how great I am, and they thank me for what I've done. Once a lady in New York City even called me a hero. That hurt. I'm not a hero, I smiled of course, and I thanked her, but I did what I had to do, and it was something that needed to be done. Not one time was I thinking to myself that the time, effort, and energy we put into Faith would bring about a book about her experiences, or that those experiences were going to be so wonderful. The book falls into its natural place after these experiences, and perhaps because of my educational background; Faith is Faith because of her own choice to live and God's grace to make it a reality. All the work in the world, all the bending over, the feeding through an eyedropper, and even the breathing into her nostrils after I stepped on her in the shower, would not have made a bit of difference in her life if she herself hadn't seen fit to stay alive. She wanted to live, and she wanted to run, she wanted to chase the geese, eat the bratsworth out of the hand of the generous man we met on Broadway who wanted nothing more than to pet the head of the famous two-legged dog. Faith wasn't aware of her fame, she was aware only of the garlic and peppered spices coming off that sandwich. She is one heck of an inspiration, and still, she is 100% dog. Something we can all take a lesson from. I think that I have learned to be more of what I was made to be, at the same time I've learned to fight my way through the harder times by letting go and letting faith take over. Ode to a dog.

The people at the *Maury Show* called us when Faith was just a year old. They wanted to do a show about miracles and felt that Faith's abilities were warranted to be brought back out to New York City and to do this particular show. To be perfectly honest, I wasn't that big of a fan of the *Maury Show* because of the usual genre of the show. Issues of civil conflict, domestic violence, secrets lovers, etc., these were the mainstay of the show, and I wasn't sure that I wanted Faith to be associated with it. I did however, agree to go if they would bring Caity with us. I wasn't going to leave her at home with her brother again, wishing she had been given the opportunity to see the Big Apple, and getting to be involved with Faith. Faith has always been Laura's dog really. Just after his dynamic rescue of Faith, Reuben had moved out of the house into an apartment and he wasn't going to be taking his beloved cat Nova, let alone a dog. Reuben is more of a cat person, which in and of itself strikes me as being unnatural, but I'll save that discussion for another book. Laura had been assigned Faith really, as Matrix was my dog, and Caity had chosen to take up with Ean. Because of her relationship with Faith Laura had been called Faith's owner on the initial KFOR-TV newscast, and we just sort of let that happen. It was true however, that the family was complete in taking turns to raise Faith. Each of us made extreme sacrifices of sleep, time, effort, and even losing our food from time to time when Faith, with her 40" nose reach has been nondiscriminatory in taking food right off of our plates, or from our hands as we aren't looking. If you aren't literally watching the dog at all times when you have food anywhere near her, she will end up with it. Again, we have pictures.

When the *Maury Show* agreed to bring Caity out with Laura, Faith and I, we were on our way again to the big adventurous city of New York City. Little did Caity realize that the great people of New York City have so much fun with Faith when she is spotted walking through Central Park or down Broadway's Time Square. Manhattan is the only borough we have actually been privileged to visit on these trips, but people from all over the area have recognized Faith because of the magnificent news coverage in the City. Faith has appeared on the front page of the paper in NYC, she's been mentioned on *Regis and Kelly*, *David Letterman*, *MSNBC*, and *CNN*. She had been featured on AOL front page, and in the Harry Potter websites. She was seen on the New York City based *Ricki Lake Show* before it was canceled, and she appeared on the nightly news during the week that the Westminster Dog Show was in town; as the cameras couldn't help themselves. The prim and proper dogs of showcase quality simply had to wait a few seconds to be admired when the yellow mutt from Oklahoma nosed in on their limelight, literally walking her way into the eyes of the New York City citizens. Calls of "Faith . . . Faith!" caught up with our ears as we strolled from 42nd to 51st on Broadway in early February 2004. A lady in dark dress, prepared to cross the street to see the Broadway production of "The Producers" had left her companion to see the two-legged wonder. She petted Faith and told me she had seen her that day on the morning news. She had told her husband that she was such a fan. I had to grin. We were standing in the middle of the sidewalk, bustling with people, people teeming out of shops like Quicksilvers, the MTV Store, Roxy, even an adult video store, people pouring out into the streets to see Faith because of the daily coverage.

At one point a woman in a wheelchair, who had recently lost both of her legs to amputation due to her severe case of diabetes was made aware of Faith's appearance. We couldn't see her or even know what she was planning to do, but in time she had wheeled herself off of the sidewalk and into the street, wheeling her way North in a southbound lane, just in order to get to us. I couldn't believe it. She was crying, tears rolling off her cheeks, and her hands shaking from being frightened of the traffic, the people cursing at her, telling her to get out of their way, honking, and waving gestures at her; but she came up to us at the intersection of 47th where there is a bit of a ramp available to her. "Faith!" She cried out and I saw her wheeling herself against the traffic which had just gotten the green light. Almost instantly I handed a police officer standing on the corner the leash I had Faith led by, I ran to the lady in the wheelchair and pushed her to the corner, up the ramp, and closer to her prize. She hadn't believed in anything she told me. She hadn't been a Christian, she hadn't been a religious person at all until after the last operation and something told her that she was not going to be around much longer. She was going to die, and there had to be a plan made for her. It wasn't until she received a burial plot advertisement in the mail that it all made sense. She took up the offer and purchased a single plot for herself. There was no one to be buried beside. There was no one who would be wanting to be buried beside her she reasoned. She had no family to speak of. Her only daughter was in another country, in France she believed. She hadn't spoken to her in years. It was an easy choice she stated because she had the money now and needed to make the plans so that her friends weren't forced to do that for her.

That morning she had decided that she might even go to the pawn store and purchase a gun. She'd have to wait a week but that didn't stop her from deciding that it was the best thing to do. She had lost all . . . faith. Before she left the house and called a taxi for help to get her to the pawn shop she had seen the

strangest thing on television. It was a rerun of the *Ripley's
Believe it or Not* show where Faith was featured, walking
tall, going in and out of the water, struggling to catch
the geese, and being loved on by a little Hispanic
boy who was blind. Faith had made a difference in
her life instantly, and she was sure that she would be
OK. Her day was spent trying to find someone who
could help her find Faith through the network she
had seen *Ripley's* on, was it Fox? Was it CBS? She
couldn't remember. The day was spent in joy, rather
than depression and it wasn't due to anything she
could explain. She told me that she laughed all day
long and that she had picked up the phone to make
a few calls to friends that she hadn't even talked to
since the operation. They didn't want to be bothered,
she had told herself. They had lives, they had families
with both legs, they had people to see, places to go.
She'd make the calls anyway, and just by fluke . . .
or maybe by faith, she was going to see one of her
friends who worked on Broadway at the Viacom
building where MTV is broadcast. She was wheeling
her way down Broadway when the muttle on the streets
was that there was a yellow two-legged dog inside of
Quicksilvers. IT COULDN'T BE! But it was. Faith
was in New York City that very day, and she was
walking up Broadway. Carolyn Gold pushed herself
to the utmost limits, because she felt she could, and
because she felt that she had to. This is what Faith

was created for. *This* was the reason Faith was given life.

I couldn't help myself, I picked Faith up and plopped her yellow butt onto the lap of this absolutely beautiful woman whose tear-streaked face never stopped kissing her for the longest of times. I didn't have my camera with me, but as is always the case in Times Square, other people had their's. Camcorders broke out, instant 35MM cameras, and digital phones caught the moments as they expressed themselves so wonderfully. I hope Carolyn was able to get a few copies for herself. I gave her our website *www.faiththedog.net* and made sure she would be added to the long and growing list of Friends of Faith if she was to e-mail us and let us know how she was doing. From the time we left Oklahoma City to the time we came home from filming the *Maury Show*, even before the show aired, over 14,000 new hits had made their way to our site. We're going to have to get a larger space I'm afraid. We had to re-do it one other time, right after Faith appeared on *Ripley's*. I suppose it has something to do with the fact that she is so novel, but it has to do more I believe, with the fact that she is such an awesome example of dogged-determination. (I couldn't help myself on that pun.) Carolyn's desire to see Faith was so strong, and that desire doesn't stop with only people who have disabilities.

Every week I receive e-mails and letters from people who own dogs, cats, and other animals with disabilities, or in some cases their beautiful pets are about to have an operation to remove one of their legs following a diagnosis of cancer or perhaps the result of an accident. One such letter came from a woman named Renee Hart in California who has a rhodesian ridgeback named Huckleberry. She wrote because Huck was about to have his right front leg amputated after a run in with a car on a road near their walnut farm. A neighbor had heard the accident and came running. Renee mentioned that people she knew and talked with had given her a great deal of advise. Some had said she should put Huck out of his misery, she should put him to sleep because of the injury. Thank God she didn't listen to them. She had heard about Faith a year or so before the accident and she had remembered how Faith's life full and exciting. She knew that dogs, like people, are resilient and if we just give our lives a chance to work out the hard situations we come across we really can overcome much more than we thought we could. Dogs are no different. We have to think about their feelings when we make decisions which will ultimately effect their lives.

After receiving Renee's letter, and a donation from her to help get my book published, I called her on the phone to see how Huck was feeling. She said he had been so agile and so up and about that he had managed to lick off his bandages, walk around, stand up and get around the house within a day or so of his operation. What a spirit! Who can hold something like that back? Faith has inspired so many people and when I think about it, I really do sit back and smile. I laugh out loud sometimes and just think how really exciting it is to be in her life . . . and then I remember; she's part of my life. God is so cool!

Chapter Eighteen

I have an English sur name, a name my sister made me promise not to tarnish in any way during the writing of this book. The name Stringfellow is not as I used to pretend it was, of Scottish heritage, it is decisively English, and with the knowledge of genealogy tidbits gathered from my sister, I can at least be sure that the first Stringfellows that we know about were literally the people who strung the instruments for the people of the great isle back in the day. We were the people you would see if your guitar strings broke. I remember telling my fifth grade teacher Mrs. Leard that the Stringfellows were the first people paid to hang people, that stringing them up had lent us the title of the "Fellow who strings". I knew I was lying when I said it, but it got me out of a horribly boring essay. In Mrs. Leard's class you could do oral reports or written ones. This was great news to a little brat of a girl with a vivid imagination.

Stringfellow is also a well known name in London, and I have to apologize to my sister at this point, and make it known that I am not the one who has given the name a rather controversial reputation. That was created by the very well off owner of at least two clubs by the name Stringfellows. There is one in London, that I know about, and still another one in New York City. I wanted to visit it while I was in the city. I wanted to flash my state license, proving my name was the same, perhaps it would have brought a smile to the face of the door keeper. Alas, I had a dog and a minor child with me at all times, and celebrity status or not, neither Faith nor one of my daughters would be admitted. Stringfellows may be controversial, but I had to bet they were at least law abiding. Still, the English connection between myself and my life, is never too far away. What does Kevin Bacon claim? Six degrees of separation?

I was standing in my college classroom teaching, minding my own business, because that is what I do. I had been teaching at Les College of Culinary Arts and Health Sciences for just over a seven weeks or so, when one of my students, a 21 year old high school graduate who had decided to wait a while before returning to the academic world, brought me a little gift. He extended his hand to show me that he had purchased a magazine. "That's nice" I said, but I wasn't quite sure what he wanted to show me. "LOOK!" he exclaimed quite clearly, "Your dog is on the front cover!" And there she was. Faith was in the corner of the magazine, standing upright, walking, and just above her head was a little voice bubble. It read: So What? As if to say "So what, I'm walking, don't all dogs walk?" I have to admit I am quite accustomed to seeing my dog on the front covers of magazines, in the middle of magazines, and even on television from time to time. I picked up a Dallas publication once when I was in Texas and saw Faith kissing my daughter Laura; one of the syndicated photos purchased by Zuma Press, a Stephen Holman special. Zuma Press has sold the photos for whatever reason, and they have been reprinted any number of times. This time, well, it was different. I didn't do it. I did not give anyone my permission to put my dog's image in a nudey magazine.

My dog was on the front cover of the London based magazine *Bizarre* whose counterpart may be something along the lines of *Maxim* in America, however, *Bizarre* has a certain dark side to it as well. There are photos of very scantly dressed women in those pouting-to-the-point-of-provocation looks of course. The magazine also has third-world photos of beatings, raids by guerrilla soldiers, and even a picture of what appears to be a terrorist act captured on film! Frame by frame disclosure of the attack in all its inglorious horror. Somewhere in the middle of the girls, the guns, and the guts, walks a little yellow dog on her two back legs. She's walking through my living room again, as always, and again I thought that I should thank my best friend Jeannie Clarke for having the wherewithal to clean the room before Stephen Holman shot those immortal photos. The church pew ads a bit of talky-talk to it as well, as we're living in Oklahoma, the capital of the Bible Belt, but no, we aren't so religious as to think we have to have a church pew in our house for any particular reason. The pew belongs to my ex-husband's sister Dee, a woman I can say without being wrong, is a wonderful person, and for all of the things she has had to put up with she has come out as beautifully as the winter rose breaking through the late February snow. She is bright, colorful, has an excellent wit and to be honest, she found the connection between *Bizarre* and Faith to be perfectly normal. I thought it was, well . . . bizarre!

"Yes, I see Faith on the cover of the magazine. Did you buy it for me?" I asked.

"Yes. But I need the money back. If you don't mind. I'm a poor student."

"Not a problem." I paid the $6.00 and took the magazine with its young, nearly naked lady on the front. Immediately the students who were in the room waiting for class to resume wanted to view the magazine. They even said it was because Faith was on the front cover but I had to laugh at them anyway. They couldn't get that look in their eyes over a little dog. I said I would let them look at it during break, but first there required just a bit of doctoring. This sounds like I am such a nerd, but I am one. I couldn't tell you the difference really between a nerd, geek, or dork, but to be sure, I am all three of these unless the involvement with computers preludes me from being a geek in its fullest. I took a black *Sharpee* pen and drew a tank top on the front cover lady. I turned the pages and began "dressing" more women, and actually coming up with some fairly decent clothing line ideas in the process. It became a game between Caity and I. She was at the college with me that day in order to type essays for students who couldn't do it. She was paid in the past by students, but I had asked them not to do that again. When I tried to return their money only one of them was forthcoming and told me what he had paid. The others claimed that Caity, and sometimes Laura, were deserving of a tip for their help. Being home schooled my daughters have had many wonderful experiences which they would not be afforded in public high school. This demonstration of compassion and assistance is one such experience. Caity and I drew ruffled clothing, straight lined clothes, Viking uniforms, and even a little grass skirted bikini for the girl with a tiny g-string on the back cover of the book. No one complained about the girls being dressed and we made up little dialogs of the girls thanking us for covering them, as they were getting cold standing on their pages without anything to cover them. It was quite fun. I then found that stapling the pages together was needed, as some of my students were taking to rubbing off the *Sharpee* coverings. Fine people, I'll take that! I stapled every page with the exception of the pages which held photos and a little news blurb about Faith and Laura. You know the photo, the one of her youthful poochy belly sticking out, and her lips in the middle of saying something with an "Oooh" sound. She hates that picture, and there it was . . . . blazen on the pages of a racy little magazine out of London.

Break was over, and it was time to get back to the basics of teaching. This particular class was behind in their points for essay, and I had decided that a little bit of extra credit was in line. Show and Tell would save the day. I was teaching Art Appreciation, a class I was not actually supposed to be teaching as I was not accredited to teach anything dealing with Art, but I was asked by the Director of Education after I was hired, to be a TEAM player. He assured me that he would *take the hit* if anything happened. Whatever that meant. I assumed he would *take the hit* as I had given the college every transcript I had earned and a copy of my professional resume and educational vitae. How could I be expected to take a hit in any event?

There I was teaching, and listening to one of my students demonstrating the art which was required for her great grandmother to make the beautiful, antique quilt that required two other people to hold up. I was minding my own business, because that is what I do, when Johnny Prat, the Director of Education

at Les College of Culinary Arts and Health Sciences,
appeared in the window of the door. He was making
a motion for me to meet him in the hallway but it did
not appear to be that urgent. I left my record book,
magazine, papers, pens, and everything else,
including my stereo and CDs there in the room.
Johnny immediately ducked his head down a bit and
began walking me down the long hallway. Without
an explanation of any sort really, he made mention
that Hollie Haggard, our College Director would be
coming along soon. Hollie and I had been in a private
meeting about thirty minutes prior to this one. She
had wanted to look at the magazine that my student
had brought to me. She laughed at me because I had
drawn clothes on the women and she commented
that it wasn't "That bad", but still, she wasn't the
least bit upset about the coverage that Faith received.

The only thing I could think of was that my
daughter Laura had been in an accident, or perhaps
Reuben had. It was just after 4:00 p.m. and I had
Caity with me. I set myself, my nerves, and my heart
for the worst. Johnny escorted me into the large
conference room and gave me a pursed lipped face.
He said he didn't want to say anything until Hollie
had made it to the room. This was going to be
something bad. I could tell. The prayers went out
immediately for Laura, for Reuben, maybe my father,
or mother. I couldn't make anything out of his face.
What came next was completely a shock.

Johnny opened the door for Hollie, who was wiping her eyes with a white tissue. Black mascara covering most of the surface in just the time she had walked presumably from her office to the conference room. What could this possibly mean? Johnny lifted his right index finger and he said to me "Jude, this is not working out". He put up his second finger and added "You have to leave." He put up his third finger, making the symbol for the number 3, and stated "Don't ask me to explain, I can't say anything more", and he put up his fourth finger and said "Good bye". Of course I asked him to explain. To my surprise, and Hollie's chagrin, Johnny stated abruptly, using his finger demonstration a second time, that I was not working out, I had to leave, he could not tell me why, and that I had to leave right then. Not one bit of it made any sense to me. Not one explanation, and when I sought one from Hollie all I got was more tears. She stuttered something about me not being used to the types of students Les was bringing in, that the college students I had taught in years past with Oklahoma City Community College, Oklahoma Baptist University, Redlands and Langston University, had been "different". She stated that some of them weren't able to do the work I had assigned. After she realized that her attempt at lying was futile, she gave it up and said "You have to go. We can't say another word." This order wasn't coming from either Johnny or Hollie. I could tell, and the meeting Hollie and I had just minutes before the class began was all washed away. No longer was I being told I was a great asset to the college, words she had barely gotten out of her mouth before she was crying in my presence, having to recant it all. She couldn't say "Good Bye" easily, and Johnny was given the duty. She couldn't even look me in the eyes. I suppose you can't when you know you're dead wrong. What was it? I wasn't told.

The minute I was released I tried to find boxes to put my office things into. Caity was in the office at this point, my office partner Peter had been dismissed. He had been told by Johny and/or Hollie that I was going to be released, and that he needed to go home. He has subsequently told me that he was ordered to leave, and that he was told not to talk to me in the future. What is up with that? Walking though the halls it became quite apparent that the rest of the administration had no idea what was going on. I could hear them rustling around gossiping, saying "No way, you've got to be kidding!" and I remember hearing the distinctive voice of Chef Kurt Bombit telling the forty some odd students I had to leave behind that he was taking them to the kitchen, and that he was sure things would be worked out. I could hear students saying "That's not true!" but I didn't know what they were talking about. Although, by elimination of topics, I could tell it had something to do with my release. Had everyone been told before me? Chef knew, the administration was told somehow, and both Hollie and Johnny were just steps in front of me when I heard them talking. Obviously, this order came from higher up the chain, but no one was willing to say a word to me.

Caity and I drove to KFOR-TV immediately to see if Brad Edwards, a journalist with a news column called "In Your Corner". He may want to run a story about it. He may want to be in my corner. After all, Oklahoma may be an At-Will state, allowing people to be fired at the will of the employer, but there still had to be some sort of protocol, a written notice, reprimand, something! Brad wasn't in, but the receptionist, a woman of some news knowledge from the years she has been working the front door, told me that she believed this was a news worthy story, and she thought that because Faith was involved (indirectly because I was not going to be able to feed my little dog without a job) she felt that I should ask Ali Myer to do the story. Faith and Ali go back a ways now.

The following day proved immeasurable in terms of evidence against the college and in my favor. Students began calling me saying various different things. One said that I was fired for being immoral. I had allowed Laura and Faith to be in the "dirty" magazine. As if I had anything to do with that story or coverage. Another student called to say that I was being released because Hollie thought I was gay.

Which was preposterous when you considered that there were at least four known homosexuals in the class. This particular student herself was gay and she said that Hollie had told another student that I was pushing my homosexual ways onto the students through the works of art we were asked to study. I dismissed this charge as Hollie and everyone else who knows me knows I am very heterosexual. I don't have animosity toward the homosexual people I know and don't know but that couldn't be the reason. It was my calling to teach. I was the TEAM player, remember? I was teaching something alright, but it was after all something I wasn't suppose to be teaching wasn't it? Who were those people I had seen in the kitchens that afternoon? Were they from the state educational boards? Were they with the accreditation people? They seemed to be hanging out in the administration offices after I was fired. It gave me cause to wonder.

When a third student confirmed that the consensus for me being fired was immorality because I had somehow "allowed" Faith and my minor daughter to be photographed and covered in *Bizarre*, I chose to contact the magazine itself. I called Matt Potter, no relation to Harry. He was the editor at the time. I explained to Matt the situation I was in because of the pictures of Faith being in his magazine. He instructed me to call an attorney. This was a few weeks after the event, and after I had obtained the information pertaining to the people in the office. They were indeed with the accreditation committees, or someone dealing with the rules and regulations of who was teaching what at Les College. I had taken the hit, as it were, that was in his own words, meant for Johnny. I was fired, in my opinion, because the administrators at the college didn't have the proper credentials to ask me to teach Art. For that matter I had taught a course in Math just a few weeks prior, and I had no more credentials to teach it than I did to teach Art Appreciation. My degrees warrant that I teach English, Humanities, Ethics, Philosophy and even an introduction course on Psychology, but I was certainly being used and played by the Director. This I was sure of. I called KFOR-TV and Ali did her magic. The story was aired and it came across as if the college, according to the students anyway, and what they were being told, fired me because Faith was in a nudey magazine. I asked her to put in the story the bit about a possibility that the college had not filed the proper papers with the state as well.

My morality was in question, for that I wanted to file a lawsuit against Les College of Culinary Arts and Health Sciences. For defamation of character, as well as for monetary loss of wages. I was told by my attorney that because I had not been employed for more than 90 days I would not have a good case. At-Will literally means that a company, in this case a school, can fire someone at will without having to meet any criteria. Where it is entirely unjust and unfair to the employee, it keeps legal costs down when employees sue for retroactive pay and such. Les got away with it, but in the end, again, because of faith that something would turn up, I got the best of it. Funny how that works out? Can we call it fate? I don't think so.

I can't sit around and let petty people and the decisions they make ultimately affect my decisions, my life or my destiny. With each day that passes since losing my job I find another reason why I probably shouldn't have aligned myself with the small college, but the students are the ones I long for. I've tried a million times to get them out of my head, but I can't. To call them by name without their permission would be wrong. Perhaps when they read this book they will know who it is that I'm talking about, but in each and every case I found a new awakening and a sharing of faith. Not to mention a sharing of Faith my dog, because I brought her to the school on more than one occasion.

One student that stands out is a little Asian woman. I'll call her Kim. She had the heart of a saddened warrior when we met. She had been through a difficult marriage, and she felt that because of her vows to stay married she was trapped. She tried to find joy in her life, and she had done so through the life and relationship she had with her little daughter. But now, it seemed that God had taken even that from her. Kim was far too shy to bring this to my attention, but one of the reasons I ask for autobiographical essays at the beginning of my courses is to get to know the students themselves. Kim was brave as she wrote the stories about her life and what it was like to hate a God that she was brought up to love. For years I have studied graphology. I'm fairly good at it too. I can look at a good sample of handwriting and if for no other reason but to entertain myself, giving me a little more insight to the author of the paragraph or two, I am able to tell some of the more deepest secrets about a person depending on what it is that they write about themselves. In Kim's case she had all but eliminated the first hump of her "M"s when she wrote words like "mine", "month" and "Mom". They were apparent more or less when the word held an "m" in the middle, words such as "time", "remember" and so forth. I could tell from the very flattened balloons of nearly every one of her "y" words, or words rather that ended in a "y", that she and been without physical touching, there wasn't the least bit of intimacy in her life; even though I knew she was a married woman. There were other indications in her writing which led me to believe that she was angry at both her mother and her father, but that her father had been the most hurtful. He had abandoned her. This I could tell through the way she curved the top part of her capital "I" and how she barely created a bottom hook for the end of the "I". No opportunities for familial love. Kim was hurting. I pulled her to the side one day and asked her if I could help pray with her. She wasn't inhibited with me. She fell into my arms crying. She was putting on the oriental face of bravery, one I had seen so often in my foreign students at Oklahoma City Community College when they had been forced to leave their native homes and to become educated in America. Lonely, making their way in a strange and incredibly harsh world, no friends, no family contact if they did not receive good marks. Why this goes on I can't tell you, because this sort of alienation of students is not isolated and it is not manipulated by only the Asian cultures. So many of my students report to me that if they don't pass "this time" their parents will disown them, they will never spend another penny on education, and words that must bring about responsibilities. Kim was hurting deeply. Tears and a gripping fist told me that she was more than tired of carrying on with her false bravado.

"Professor Jude, I am crying. I am hurt. This hurt." she sobbed.

"Tell me Kim, what is happening?".

"My daughter, Professor, my little baby she has diabetes. I don't ask God much. I don't. I mad at Him. He make my baby sick. He make my baby to die soon." her English barrier apparent, but beautifully articulated through her love for her daughter.

"Kim, we don't always know why God allows things that seem bad to happen to beautiful and innocent people, children, or the elderly. There has to be a reason. Let me pray with you."

"He not listen. I pray. I pray every day. She is sick and I can't make it better."

"Let me pray anyway, maybe where two hearts are gathered."

I told Kim what I found in her writings. Not what I had read in the words about her favorite color, food, why she was taking classes at the Culinary college, or why she wasn't in her country anymore. I told her what I read in the innuendos of the letters themselves. Her breakdown was complete. She wanted to stay in my office and cry, and I held her. I think I held her for about an hour. We prayed together. We prayed not only for her daughter but for her own faith, her joy, she wanted the joy to return.

I have a new friend for life. I can walk away from Les, and Les can walk away from me, but forever and that last day I have a true and genuine friend named Kim. Before I was fired she was seen holding my arms as I walked down the hallways leading to the kitchens where she would finally let me go, but not before she would kiss my cheek and whisper in my ear that she loved me. She also told me to check out the bottoms of her "y" words. She had been making amends with her husband as well. There was a certain *JOY* returned that had not shadowed the bedroom for nearly a year. Kim was more than happy about her new promises from God. She told me over and over again that every day she has found the miracle. The miracle, she would say. The miracle. I can only imagine what a burden she must have let go of. I hope it had something to do with her eternal desire to be a Believer again. I'll miss Kim for sure, the administrators told the students that they were not allowed to call me. If they were caught they would be expelled from the school. Kim took the time to tell me that much before she said she could not keep a secret long and that if we were to talk she would want to tell everyone.

I'm going to be honest and say that I'm going to miss the pot heads that smoke their weed every day just before coming to my class. Without them the class would be different. In some ways the class would be more orderly, yes, but it would not have the flair of youthful rebellion that these two brought. You never knew what you were going to get when you asked a question of one or the other of these two. In their defense, neither had graduated from high school, having been too high or sleepy to attend on a regular basis. Both had been beaten by fathers, step fathers, siblings, and in one's case, a neighbor, who subsequently had raped him at the age of 14. I read this again in his writings, but not because it showed up in a curly cue, he flat out told me. I couldn't understand his candor, but this was what

Hollie had meant when she told me that these students, some of them, were not the same as the others. They told me things. They put it out there for the world to see, almost daring me to disapprove. I never did. I think they found that the most interesting part of our teacher-student relationship. I couldn't be bought off for a good grade, and I couldn't be embarrassed easily. Though there was that one time when one of my cross-dressers asked me to join him at the club after class. I think I would have loved to have watched him strut his stuff for the runway, but I declined. You never know what that sort of thing can do for the reputation of the college if a teacher openly supports such a controversial event. Little did I know that just having someone take your dog's picture could be such a problem. I held the hand of another student when she got her tummy pierced. She cornered me after class and asked me if I would be her pseudo mother. I told her I would not sign anything. I squeezed her hand harder than she squeezed mine, and it was her belly getting punctured. I watched another get married in a boat. I watched another one ride a horse in a rodeo, and took another student home after he had too much to drink once, at the school! Another time, he and I spotted each other at a restaurant over the weekend. He felt comfortable enough to ask, and even if it was the wrong thing to do, I felt it was the right thing to do. I helped him walk up the stairs, and asked his roommate to take good care of him. Twice I had taken him home, and twice I remember thinking he had too much to offer to give it up in booze. Nothing was said on Monday. Nothing happened. Teachers are often much more than a class room figurehead. I knew that. I missed the college students at Les more than I missed some of the others because the others seemed to have more opportunities. More life chances. I may become a writer and write for the rest of my life, but I will never give up teaching. It seems to be what I am, not what I do. I don't always know exactly what it is that the students are expected to learn. With Les I was teaching a course in Math where I was sure that most of the students had a better working knowledge of what it meant to divide a decimal; however, teaching isn't about being right all the time, or about setting an example every time either. Sometimes its about being where you need to be, where you are needed, and being available. Teachers have it better. I know I feel that way about teaching and when I'm in the middle of a conference with a kid who for the first time isn't able to depend on anyone other than himself or herself for the work; I remember the best teachers I have ever had. They come to mind immediately. Faithfully. Joyfully. I want to be like them. Let me be that teacher, I ask. The one they remember when *they* want to remember a teacher. Bring my face to their mind. Bring my smile back to them.

Journal Entry:

February 3, 2004:

I've decided to stay home for the next six weeks and write the book *With a Little Faith*. If I get hired I get hired. But I'm going to try to write this anyway. It needs to get written. I need this. I need to dive head deep into writing and to get a publisher. I need to write. I need to write a poetry book too, but this book comes first. If I can get this done I can make a good effort at becoming an author. If I can find a publisher I can get an advance. I'll work on the book from 7 to noon. I'll get up at 6:00 a.m. and pray, read a few lines from St. Augustine and drink my morning coffee. I have to do this.

Well, I did get up, pray and drink my morning coffee, but it was more or less around 9:30 or so. What happened to the early morning hours were predictable. I can't even imagine why I thought I could lie to myself. I don't wake up early. What was that all about? I think my idea of work is getting up early, putting my best effort forward, and getting it done. The trouble with that way of thinking is that it works for others but not for me. The alarm goes off at 6:00 a.m. just like its suppose to, but my head is reminded that I didn't get to bed before 1:30 the night before because I was reading the latest William Bernhardt thriller. I can't put it down! Bernhardt is a great deal better than Grisham if you ask me. He's funny, he's witty, and . . . he's from Oklahoma City. He and I actually worked at the same law firm, but not at the same time. I was fired from that one too, but only because I refused to back down to the Queen of the joint when she demanded that I use a certain font and I explained to her that the attorney I worked for preferred otherwise. Queens always win.

What I can do is start earlier I told myself, maybe stop writing around 7:00 p.m. so that I can pick Bill's books up a little earlier, but then I would have to start my writing some time before 11:00 a.m. since I usually go about eight hours at a stretch, and that would require that I got up earlier than . . . . this isn't' going to work. Besides, I tell myself nearly every day; if the dog is laying on my legs and she's made that sigh, that noise that indicates that she simply cannot be disturbed, who am I to wake her up and force her to do more? She's a celebrity! I'm just, well, the owner.

Chapter Nineteen

Faith seems to be showing up on all sorts of magazines these days. I saw her in a few last month and thought to myself, "Hey, they didn't ask my permission. I could be fired!" and then I laughed. I'm not working! Her image has become somewhat of a public domain. She could be marketed I suppose, perhaps I will get a license to make Faith dolls, magnets, notebooks, or posters. I think one of Laura's friends said there are Faith posters in Germany, but I have not seen any evidence of this. Faith isn't about making money or being the next *Benji*. She has a completely different calling, one she hasn't given much thought to I'm afraid. She lays about the house and expects me to make those types of decisions for her. She will be the one to show up, smile, putting her ears back up on the top of her head and walk from one end of the block to the other to show off her abilities to do it. Some dogs grab a raggedy ball and tempt you with it, trying to pull you into their game. Faith is more likely to take off out the front door and

stand outside the car until you open the door letting
her in. She loves to ride, and she loves to hang her
head out the window slobbering on the passengers
in cars behind us. She is such a dog at times! We'll
be standing in line at the airport waiting to get our
baggage scanned and trying to look all proper like.
This isn't a time to be silly and bite the cords of the
scanners, but there she was in Newark! I had to
apologize. "That's OK, we know Faith!" I was happy
to see a friendly face because her next dog-like
activity had more to do with the fact that flying four
hours and waiting in the airport an additional two
hours before that, led me to understand why dogs
are usually carted and placed in the plane's
enormous belly.

If pooping in the airport wasn't illegal before, I'm
sure I'll soon see signs that say "Do Not Poop in the
Airport" posted at the terminal gates. Where is a plastic
baggie when you need it? We had just left the airplane
in Dallas for a connecting flight to Oklahoma City
when Laura felt a definite pull on her arm. Faith just
couldn't wait any longer. I tried not to laugh, but
honestly, pooping on Texas! This was so . . . .
Oklahoman! My dog was a true Crimson and Cream
(yellow) Sooner! I had to write to Coach Stoops about
it, and of course, I cleaned up the mess. You haven't
lived until you're asked to sign autographs seconds
after you've mopped up a mess like that! "For her
next performance, Faith will be doing stand up at the

Improv!" I made my way onto the plane to an eruption of applause. We Okies do like our little ironies you know. The idea of Faith choosing Texas to releave herself did not escape any of us. Even a few die hard Longhorn fans found it hilarious. "When a girl's gotta go, a girl's gotta go" was one of the more lively comments.

Big Dog Sports contacted us again through their Marketing Director Margaret Dunbar. She was yet another person who just happened to run across another story about Faith in a national magazine. She told me that she had never seen a dog with more courage, and that she wanted Faith to be, what she called, a "leader of the pack" for Big Dog Sports. There wasn't much time to plan a trip to California for Faith to be in the parade, and so the hope was that Faith would show her support for Big Dog by wearing t-shirts and bandannas with Big Dog logos. Big Dog also ran a little story about Faith in their Christmas catalog, stating that one of Faith's endeavors is to go where disabled children are so that she can be an inspiration. They mentioned Faith's "paw-sitive" attitude and for that we're very thankful. Big Dogs Sports' people aren't the only ones who can't get enough of Faith. I mentioned *Bizarre* Magazine earlier; since her first steps on television in June of 2003, Faith has appeared in more than 60 magazines, on more than 24 television shows, and has been talked about by millions. I tell my students that you'd think

I would be a millionaire by now, flying around the world with Faith doing shows and talking to people who need a little encouragement. It hasn't happened yet. In fact, it's quite the opposite.

Chapter Twenty

September 2004 was a great time for publicity for Faith. Someone had placed a faux story on a Harry Potter website about Faith being in the next movie. The movie they were talking about was the Goblet of Fire. I was just as surprised as anyone when I woke up and prepared myself to go to work, (by this time I had been employed by the Oklahoma City Public School District as a 9th grade English teacher) to find a host of television news vans parked outside my little house. When they began asking me about Goblet of Fire I was completely caught off guard. I had an attorney for Faith, but I had not been told whether or not we would be invited to be in a movie. I was certainly excited about any possibility of Faith being in a Harry Potter film. Wow, that would be really cool.

I could just about imagine Laura, my red-head, being so prim and proper on the set, while trying her hardest to get a look-see at Rupert Grint. They would instantly fall in love of course, and he would be completely swept away with her because she not only looked quite a bit like Lindsay Lohan, she was intelligent, liked anime, could hold her own in a conversation, and she was, after all, the owner of the world's only two legged dog Faith. This was a dream of course, but one worth dreaming. I had to explain to the news media that I was not at liberty to discuss the matter as I had not discussed it with my attorney. This bit of information led the media hounds to run off to their word processors and camera people and to state that I knew I would be in the film, and then all sorts of stories began hitting the internet, the papers, the magazines, and of course international news stations. Fox ran a great story about it, I asked Phyllis Williams of our local media to run the story herself. Because I didn't know if the story was valid or not I took it upon myself not to find out until a bit of coverage had been reported. It can't hurt to have the possibility thrown out there for someone with authority to take the news and run with it. It just might pan out. After the story hit CNN and other national and international headlines, we were told that the people of Birds and Animals Unlimited, the trainers for all of the Harry Potter films, were talking about the possibility of the use of Faith in one of their films, but it was the New York office doing the pushing we were told, not the British branch of the company, as they were determined to keep all of the Potter films British right down to the last actor, even if it was a dog. This of course, didn't work out for them as the panthers in the movie Faith may have been in are not from Britain at all, and they were not trained there either. So, that leaves a door open doesn't it? Perhaps Faith can be in the next film, but I won't hold my breath. If she is, she is. Faith has more to do than act in movies, she has people to see and faces to kiss. The summer of 2005 found my son Reuben playing as an extra in a independent film called Wisteria, the story of an evil older man from New York named Albert Fish. Fish used to kidnap children and actually eat them. The film was being filmed in a city near where we lived, and on a whim we took Faith down to see the casting crew. Faith wasn't picked, as it was a very serious film, however, Reu plays the part of a city cop. During the filming of the movie I had the opportunity to bring Faith onto the set for a little brevity among the crew. One of the best decisions I could have made for a lazy summer. Faith was immediately loved by everyone on the set especially a really interesting actor by the name of Vyto Ruginis. Ruginis has been a million things, and if anyone were to look him up on the internet, they would find that he is a seasoned character actor. The role he plays in Wisteria is that of a police detective in the late 1920's and early 1930's as Fish was being sought by authorities.

Vyto, sometimes in costume, sometimes out of costume, would sit on the grass beside Faith and I and we'd talk about film making, about people and the way they handle certain situations. "Faith for instance", offered Vyto. "She doesn't know she's different does she? She walks, she barks, she eats, she chases squirrels, just like a regular dog. But Faith has a message that anyone can understand. You have to try in life, you have to do things for yourself." I truly appreciated what Vyto had to say about my dog, and he was truly touched by the way Faith made her day to day life seem seamless. She wasn't acting like a diva, or something special, she was . . . and she is, a dog.

It was through the filming of Wisteria that Faith and I met an attorney from Washington D.C. When he came out of a local nursing home where his mother was a resident. As he wheeled his mother out of the home in her wheelchair it became apparent to me that both he and she were staring at my dog. Being rather used to people staring at Faith, I stood up from the grassy patch I was resting on and began walking over to them. They weren't alone, a former mayor of the City of Guthrie was with them, as well as her sister. It seemed a small group had gathered by the time we made it over to the attorney and his mother. Amazed and full of questions I tried to answer as much as I could about Faith for them, and just as she always does wherever she goes, Faith was able to make a new bridge between my life and the life of someone who would be working with me in the future in terms of formulating Faith's career. Clif McCann, the attorney e-mailed me after seeing Faith's website and suggested we have the name of Faith the Dog made into a trademark to protect her from anyone in the future using her image for anything less than admirable. Who would have thought? I would never have imagined a couple of years ago that holding a little two legged dog in my hands, trying to make her stand up and walk, would lead to me needing a trademark in order to protect her rights. I didn't even realize dogs had rights! Hey, everyone . . . dogs have rights!

Before the fun and excitement of filming a critically acclaimed independent film, where my role was very interesting: I was the personal assistant to an extra, I had been employed by an Oklahoma City Public school where things were not always as they seemed. It didn't take long to figure out that it was going to take a great deal of faith, the ordinary kind, just to survive the twists and turns of this ride.

I was employed for only one year, the term would be terminal I was told. I was not expected to come back, it was not a matter of me being a bad teacher, but the district had a way of making teachers apply for their own jobs year after year, and this particular position was a new one, one that would probably not be made available the next year, or any other year subsequent. It was months before I realized that the school I was working at was under the government's eye. They were being scrutinized for having one of the lowest ranking test scores in the state, and because of the massive turnovers in administration over the past few years, a new principal had been hired. He was from another state, he was going to make things happen, he was going to turn things around. He ran into the brick wall that is secondary education in the inter city schools of Oklahoma City. At least I had the comfort of knowing that whenever I was being screamed at by an administrator it wasn't always something I was responsible for. Sometimes, as it turned out, it was the fact that the scores were too low, the English Second Language students too many, and the expectations of bringing up benchmarks, advanced performance indexes, and other standardized scores was simply an impossibility. The school is still on its way out at the time of this press, however, the faith shown by the students to continue to try and to continue to want to be educated amazes me. Not everyone wants to be taught, I'm not so naïve to believe that the school I taught at was one of the schools imitated in the movies where principals, teachers, and students work together to pull out of the slump that time has created. This school had the makings of a success story, unfortunately for the district, the superintendent and the principal himself are not living in reality. Times do change, but not over night.

On the afternoon of February 28, 2004, I was in my classroom, we were working on Romeo and Juliet, a standard for any 9th grade class. We had seen the movie, and we were discussing it when over the PA system our 11th grade vice principal made the announcement that the student body could be released to go to the gym for the Brotherhood Assembly. This was going to be a great celebration of all of the mixed cultures of our school. My favorite two events were going to be the rap hip-hop sounds of a student who is only 4'6" tall, and he's Hispanic. He is so funny and so much fun to know. He can rap! He can dance! He was going to be really outstanding. The second group that was really on my mind were the stomp group. A group of African American girls from all grades who had been working hard on a skit which included a plot as well as their stomp dances. I couldn't wait.

The announcement to dismiss came a bit early according to my estimation, but that was nothing new. If one thing was sure about this school, it was that nothing went as planned. Nothing was as it seemed, nothing was done the way it was suppose to be done, but we the teachers had better follow any and every directive given. This announcement was a fool's folly. Every student exited without order to the halls, scampering, running, trying to get the best seats, or simply trying to get out of the building and off of the grounds without being caught. Like I said, it was a normal school with normal kids attending it.

About five minutes, a full five minutes after the first announcement was made, our 11th grade vice principal made a second announcement when he realized what his first call to dismiss resembled. "Teachers", he implored, "At this time, please only release the students who are to be a part of the Brotherhood Assembly". Right! Oh yes, let's just go into the crowded massive halls of the school and somehow, because we're miracle workers, call to order the groups and throngs of heads and feet that are bobbing through the corridors at this time. Perhaps we will even be able to be heard over the laughing, screaming, yelling, radios, cell-phones calling, and locker doors slamming. That didn't happen. I managed to wrangle four.

Another full five minutes goes by and the same lazy-lipped principal calls out one more time. "Teachers, at this time, please escort your students to the assigned areas of the auditorium where you normally sit." WHAT? What on Earth is this man talking about? We didn't have assigned seats. We didn't normally go to the assemblies at this time, even if we did have normal assigned seats, it would not be for this group of students. We were in third block I believe, and we normally had assemblies during fourth.

Suffice it to say that the panic that was once among the halls was now billowing its way into the orifices of the grand auditorium. As my class was upstairs I believed my non-assigned assigned seats would be upstairs. I was wrong. Of course I was wrong. I couldn't possibly expect this school do have any realism. Not after all the years it ran so well in complete chaos. I walked the four students I managed to corral into the auditorium on the top level of the school where I met with another English teacher, one who will not be named. She mentioned to me that she believed I was to be downstairs, and that she would check it out if I were to watch her area and not let anyone sit in it. I did exactly what I was told. That's just it. I always did exactly what I was told, but I was never really quiet about it. I usually made a comment about it being ridiculous to one or another of the other older teachers, who usually had another comment to the same effect to me. This was our way of venting without being completely terrible about it.

As I stood there guarding her area I was accosted, literally stepped on by my own vice principal who felt that it was her duty to yell in my face, causing her own spit to hit me squarely in the eye. As I tried to wipe it off, I also tried to understand her ranting over the music, the drums, the announcements from the stage, and the hundreds, now nearly a thousand kids seated on the second level. She was muttering something about me being downstairs, and that I had no right to be in the other teacher's area. When I tried to explain my position to her, I was awarded more spit. This exchange was witnessed of course, not only by other teachers, but a wonderful ROTC Sgt. Major, who refused to allow it to go on. Calling to my vice principal by name, he told her to back off, to stand down, and she did not. He told her once more that he would not allow her to mistreat me. She finally backed off of my foot and I breathed a frightful breath. I was so upset about what had just taken place that I immediately went down to the office to place a call to my union representative Rick, who I had been very accustomed to calling.

When I reached the office I was told by one of the three secretaries that I had a call, it would be patched through to the visitor's phone by the front door. I took the call. It happened to a news reporter from the Oklahoman, our city's largest paper. He wanted to do a story on Faith. I told him I had another story for him, one that would be amazing to his readers about the district and the way that teachers were being man-handled at the school. He was very interested, so interested in fact, that he put me on hold while he got another tape to record my every word. It wasn't long before my vice principal and the 11th grade vice principal had found me. I think they were actually looking for me. I could hear the music from the auditorium and knew that the assembly had started. Their real position at this time should have been monitoring the students, but here they were on a witch hunt, looking for their stray teacher who they had reason to believe was calling the union to file a formal complaint. Let me just say that the reporter, as well as myself, got two ears full when the 9th grade vice principal was in my face again, this time without the accoustics of the music filled auditorium to block out what she was screaming. Every eye of everyone in the office was bulging and staring at us. I simply turned the phone toward her mouth and let the reporter do his job. He wanted me to spell her name, and right there in front of God and everyone, I did. When I completely ignored her she became enraged. She was stepping over every professional boundary there was, but with the main principal out of the school, she felt that as supervising principal she had the right to belittle, berate, humiliate, and cause as much disturbance as was humanly possible. With her 6'2" frame, I wasn't sure she was actually human, but believed her to be some sort of Amazon from another world.

When the dust settled I returned to my classroom, where I picked up my purse, my lunchbox, and I left the building. I signed out, I said good bye to the ladies in the office, and I smiled at the main principal's secretary Shirley. She's the nicest person in the entire school, and I wanted her to see that I was not ruffled. She smiled back, shook her head, and said "Ms. Stringfellow, you do get yourself into trouble!" I answered back "Just doing my job!" As I had been in scuffs with the administration since the first day of school when it was very clear that following the laws and the proper procedures of ethics in a public institution of education was not on their minds.

Someone had to stand up for the kids. This took faith, a little moxie too, I knew I would not be coming back, but I had no idea I would be asked to leave early.

On March 3, 2005, I was escorted from my room the second the last bell rang. Here stood the Amazon and the main principal with a mandated letter from the former asking me to leave and not return. Not until a formal hearing on the matter could be held. This formal hearing was scheduled for the last week of the year. My students, over 100 of them, would be given substitutes, less than educated persons without the reasonable responsibility to see to it that the advanced performance indexes, the benchmarks, and the standardized scores of the students were brought up. They were babysitters and they were bad at that from what I was told.

At the hearing I was vindicated. I was told that she was wrong, that she had no right to do what she was doing, naturally I assumed this meant that I would be given a chance to return and see to it that the next year would be a better year. I was wrong. I was asked not to return as I was causing too much of a problem when I let the union know, and the state of Oklahoma know that the school district and the school administrators were not following standard operating standards of what is expected at an inter city high school. I was guaranteed that my file would be sealed. I was told that I would be paid, I was told that I would receive the insurance benefits, and that I would be given the standard reference that anyone received if anyone called for a performance or personal reference. Faith is a funny thing. I was expected to show faith in the same district that treated me so badly. I was expected to show faith in the very people that lied to me, spat on me, and even wrongfully walked me out of the building in front of hundreds of students who wondered if I were being arrested for something. Faith is a funny thing. I had to show it, it was this moment that I chose to be quiet, and to let the actions of the administration be seen by the students who knew me too well to know that I would never do anything illegal. They knew. They had faith too, but it wasn't in their school, it was in me. I had to be strong and I had to let them go.

Chapter Twenty One

The summer of 2005 found me in quite the bind again, as I faced the hard cold facts that telling the truth to people who don't relish being truthful can cost a person much more than they ever expected. My Dad used to say that I speak my mind even when my mind should shut up. He's right, I don't hold back what I'm thinking and although it is most likely the truth that I'm speaking, I have had to learn to speak less and save more. I interviewed with quite a few school districts over the summer months of 2005, and in every case I was called back for a second, and sometimes a third interview. It was obvious to me that the administrator liked what I had to offer in terms of being a high school teacher, but for reasons unknown, I was never hired. I received a letter or a phone call, in one instance I received an e-mail, all stating that they were choosing another candidate to fill the position of being their needed English teacher for the upcoming year. I knew something was going on, something sinister such as my previous employer telling tales about me, or perhaps telling more than is legally allowed when an employer calls for a reference. It's easy to do really, and no one would be the wiser. Trying to prove that you've been talked about by a previous employer is about the hardest thing in the world to do. You can't record the conversations being held between two parties you don't even know are talking to one another. It would be easy for one party to say to the other "Hey, buddy, I know I'm not suppose to ask, but . . . what kind of an employee was Jude anyway?"

My mouth has gotten me into more trouble by speaking the truth about a situation than it ever has by speaking a lie. For instance, at the Oklahoma City Public School that I worked at in 2004, I was very open and very honest about the fact that my administrator had stepped on my foot and that she had spat on my face while she was barking at me. I had mentioned it to the principals where I was interviewing that I had need to involve my union. The kind-hearted secretary told me about a week after I had been asked to leave, that the same administrator that had spat on me had physically grabbed one of my students by the back of the neck and forced him into the wall. This woman, the administrator, takes matters of control into her own hands and uses her size and her position as an intimidation mechanism. The boy may have been afraid of her, but I was not. I immediately called the parents of the kid to let them know. They stated to me that because they were illegally in this country they were not going to bring the administrator to any form of justice. Through broken English they thanked me for caring, but asked me not to contact them further as the school had already "warned" them against talking with me. While checking my history or my background at this particular school, it wouldn't be very hard for a new employer to find out this sort of information. I was literally the only teacher that I remember who was stupid enough or strong enough to stand up to the woman that called herself a leader of the school, to let her know that she would be held accountable someday for what she mistook as power or authority. My mouth gets me into trouble, yes, and my pen records its for life. I have more than 300 journals which I have kept on a near daily basis since I was quite small. Using about 20-25 composition notebooks a year now, I'm sure I'll reach over 1,500 before I'm finished. When I die, I have asked my friend Victoria Reddling, my counselor and spiritual leader, to go through them and to publish the parts that could be published without embarrassing my family too much. She is also to ask my friend Will Orr if he wants his name to be published in a book that I have written, and if he does, she is to ask him if he wants his name to be changed to Bill or something. For that matter, several friends should be consulted before I mention them in books without their permission. Wouldn't it be best to ask David Parker, a man who is like an uncle to Reuben, if he would want to be in the book? After all ink on the printed page can be very loud. Ink can be deafening when it needs to be, and my experiences at Oklahoma City Schools is not only recorded, it is recorded in detail, I should give the same consideration to my friends, lest they pretend they don't know me when I meet them on the streets.

Faith is a multi-faceted thing. You have to have it in order to see yourself through to the end of whatever it is that you're planning to do. I needed a job, I had to have one, it wasn't as if my kids could feed themselves, nor could my mortgage be paid simply by hoping . . . hope is great, I hoped a great deal, but faith is the only thing that truly gets me through these times. I guess I can best explain it by adding another word to the mix; work. You can't just have faith, you have to work at whatever it is that you want. Let's say I wanted a job. I did want a job. I had to have one. I could sit on my butt and wait for the phone to ring, which would be more indicative of hope, or I could get up, buy the paper, go through the classifieds, circle the ads that I would be qualified for, make the calls, go on the appointments, tell my side of my story, thank the manager . . . and . . . pray. I also have to work. I have to build a resume, take that resume to the places I want to work. Set up interviews, show up for interviews. I can't just hope or want to be hired. Faith without work, according to the Bible, is dead. I don't want dead. I want life. Life is good. Have you ever sat at home and stared at the phone because it was suppose to be ringing for you? The person on the other end, say a friend, doesn't realize you're about to pounce the receiver when they call. When they call, and you pounce, they seem so surprised to hear you utter in disappointment "Oh, it's you. I was hoping it was someone else." Oh goody, now you're upset and you've just upset your friend as well. No, I think faith, the real faith is just waiting normally for the phone or the letter in the mail asking you to come to work, or telling you that whatever it was that you wanted has happened. You have to put forth the right effort, do the right things, and dot the i's as you cross your t's, but you don't have to worry. Faith, well, faith is when you do what you have to do, you call on whomever it is that can make it happen, and you just let it happen. Hard? You bet it is. It's the hardest thing in the world because you can't control fate, but you can . . . and you should, control faith.

I've been drawn out, held out, freaked out, and made to question my own faith a million times, but the truth is, my time is simply not God's time. Looking back, OK, having 20-20 site, I can see where being God is something I just wouldn't want to do. He's really got a tough job, and asking me to show a little faith in Him is not that big of a deal. He's never let me down . . . and if that sounds corny, or churchy, you'll have to forgive me. I'm a little corny and I'm a little churchy from time to time. (Don't read every page of my journal if you're thinking you'd like to put me on some sort of a pedestal though, you'll soon find out that I'm a lot like you.) Have you ever had to wait for something and you really didn't think you had the time to do it? If you're like me you grab the notebook, scratch out all the things you have to do, things you have to pay right now, things you can't get away with not paying, or not doing. If you're like me you can't find the time, the money, the resources, or the information you need to get the job done, but you can't stop either. Stopping would mean giving up, and if there's one thing I do better than speaking my mind, it's holding on. I could be a bulldog I suppose.

Thinking in terms of what is next for Faith I'll be honest with you and say that she should be seen by as many people as she can be. Whether that is through commercials, movies, music videos, or just being on the covers of magazines and newspapers, Faith is meant to be there to help people who otherwise have difficult times in their ordinary lives. When we go to places to talk about our mission, places like the Angel Tree in Bethany, Oklahoma, a place where kids whose parents are incarcerated, we talk about hope. We talk about what God can do for anyone, you, me, Faith, and others who are willing to put forth the effort in their lives to stand up and do the walking. Walking by faith, not necessarily on two legs. Carolyn Gold wheeled herself to us. I'm talking about putting on the protection of faith, and doing whatever it is necessary to fight the battles using wisdom, and hope, prayer, and others as your weapons. The actions of doing so is the product of faith. Faith really is the substance of things hoped for. Substance meaning, the thing which that hope or dream is made of. Getting up and making things happen is only part of it. Being willing to work for the goal, being willing to be there for someone else whose goals are being met, and in doing so, perhaps even further your own set of goals in a direction you never dreamed of. Faith is the evidence of things not seen. Can you see it? Take a walk with me someday down the streets of a really crowded city, on the moving sidewalks in the airport, up the escalators at the malls, or maybe down the hallways of a nursery school, hospital wing or community center. When you do, watch the people as they see the laughing little yellow dog. They lose something when they do. They lose their fear of the day, they lose their burdens, they drop the very thought that was bothering them just a few minutes before. For them, this moment is all there is. And in that moment, they see faith in the body of a miracle. They see Faith.

After Thoughts

This book was written and ready to go at the end of Spring 2005. It was at that time that I was told by the Oklahoma City Schools that I would be receiving a lump sum pay out for the contract we had signed in August of the following year. Strangely, just two days before the call came from the district telling me that I would be paid, I was released from the only position of employment I had regarding teaching at the college level as well. Budget cuts again? I wondered. However, I had already signed a contract with the college as well, and demanded that my pay not be affected by their decision to release several instructors. I was the only instructor paid for the summer months who had been released. Something in my head had told me days before to go to the school and to sign my contracts. It wasn't a phone call, or a mailed notice, it was a voice in my head and my heart warning me that it was the thing to do. I'm glad I listened.

The film *Wisteria* comes out in October 2006. You should be warned that it is a bit on the gritty side, however, Vyto and my son make the film worth going to see no matter how you feel about gritty tales.

Faith has her own website. It was set up by Matt Layne, a fantastic man, a fan of Faith's, and great webmaster. He is with Timeline.com and is wise and talented beyond belief. I decided to add a blurp on the website about needing help to get the book published. It worked. In the front of this book I mention the names of the people who graciously, generously, and wonderfully, without self thought, gave to the project, but I can't leave that alone. I want to be sure and thank them one more time. Thank you Debbie Minshall and family, Ginger and Dennis Handy, Ericka from Seattle, and Xlibris for the finished project of this book. Greg Haigh at Xlibris has been with me throughout the whole mess as I have anguished to get the book finished. He has been amazing. Ginger Handy gets a SECOND thank you because she, the crazy woman, bid on an auction I held on Ebay and she won the "Thank You" in the book. She already had a thank you! But, for Ginger, you can never say it enough. Thanks AGAIN. Thank you to the readers who have found this book an inspiration, thank you to my kids who have let me have the time to write without being interrupted . . . . too much. Thank you Faithy, I call her Yellow Dog most of the time now. She is truly an act of God.

Printed in the United States
77923LV00004B/280-312

9 781425 718497